I0488265

THE *Perfect* LAST IMPRESSION

Also by Tom and Jeanne Emanuel

HOW TO BE A SUCCESSOR TRUSTEE
ED AND EDITH CREATE A LIVING TRUST

THE *Perfect* LAST IMPRESSION

The Art of Leaving More Than Just Money to Your Heirs

A. Jeanne Emanuel, J.D.

Thomas A. Emanuel, M.A.

Authors of *How To Be a Successor Trustee* and *Ed and Edith Create a Living Trust*

iUniverse, Inc.

New York Lincoln Shanghai

The Perfect Last Impression
The Art of Leaving More than Just Money to Your Heirs

Copyright © 2007 by Great Times LLC, a Nevada LLC

All rights reserved. No part of this book may be used or reproduced by any means, graphic, electronic, or mechanical, including photocopying, recording, taping or by any information storage retrieval system without the written permission of the publisher except in the case of brief quotations embodied in critical articles and reviews.

iUniverse books may be ordered through booksellers or by contacting:

iUniverse
2021 Pine Lake Road, Suite 100
Lincoln, NE 68512
www.iuniverse.com
1-800-Authors (1-800-288-4677)

Because of the dynamic nature of the Internet, any Web addresses or links contained in this book may have changed since publication and may no longer be valid.

The information, ideas, and suggestions in this book are not intended to render legal advice. Before following any suggestions contained in this book, you should consult your personal attorney. Neither the author nor the publisher shall be liable or responsible for any loss or damage allegedly arising as a consequence of your use or application of any information or suggestions in this book.

ISBN: 978-0-595-42542-6 (pbk)
ISBN: 978-0-595-86870-4 (ebk)

Printed in the United States of America

We dedicate this book to those courageous souls who understand its message and dare to leave the perfect last impression.

CONTENTS

ACKNOWLEDGMENTS

This book could not have been written without the caring thought and the warm wisdom of the hundreds of clients whom we have been fortunate to work with in the estate planning business. We wish to acknowledge the stories they have given us, and although we did not use their real names, they really helped to clarify the message we have tried to deliver in this book. We are most grateful for their support and the confidence they have shown in us.

WE WANT TO THANK OUR FAMILIES—JEANNE'S SON BRUCE, HIS WIFE STACY AND THEIR CHILDREN, WENDY AND BRANDON; JEANNE'S DAUGHTER KIM, HER HUSBAND DAN, AND THEIR BOYS, CLARK AND KYLE; TOM'S DAUGHTER ASHLEY AND HER HUSBAND CHRIS; HIS PARENTS, BETTY AND LEONARD; HIS BROTHER, PETER, AND SISTERS, JEAN AND BARBARA; AND ALL THEIR FAMILIES—HAVE ALL CONTRIBUTED IN LOVING WAYS OVER MANY YEARS TO BRING US TO THE POINT WHERE WE COULD WRITE A BOOK LIKE THIS. We love them all dearly and want them to be proud of us for passing on their great gifts to our readers.

Finally, we want to send heartfelt encouragement to all loving people who are struggling to find a way to express their love and their last wishes appropriately to their children and their heirs. We dedicate whatever knowledge and strength we have to that effort.

FOREWORD

Frankly, we were mystified when Jeanne and Tom approached us about writing a foreword for *The Perfect Last Impression*. We write about love, about relationships, about improving self-image—not about estate planning and the law. Somehow, we thought, we're inappropriate for this task.

Then we read the manuscript. What a fabulous, beautiful approach! We loved the idea of injecting true value, love, and the importance of emotional gifts we leave our heirs into the dry legal process of estate planning! We felt thrilled and honored to write the foreword.

The Perfect Last Impression truly is all about love—love for children, love for family, and love for friends. It's a wonderful, stimulating, positive approach to the transferring of an estate. Along with divorce law, this area of law has often been one that has caused the most family havoc and heartache. The emotional and economic costs over the years have been truly incalculable! Finally, here is a book with a tremendously valuable solution.

If you have any interest at all in estate planning, this is a must book for you. Not only does this book explore and advocate new and refreshing ideas about what it really means to "provide for your heirs," it is by far the clearest expression that we have ever come across of how this complicated and intricate area of law really works. It is a reference book, a practical planning book, an impetus to "do something" book, and a wise and loving guide to treating your family right—all rolled into one.

We have done some estate planning ourselves. But until we read this book we never understood in such a crystal-clear manner what impact our actions would have on our loved ones. This book contains profound insights that the authors have related through a multitude of meaningful—sometimes amusing, sometimes sad—examples from actual clients. Through these real-life examples they have succeeded brilliantly in illuminating our options in a way that entices us to action in an area that, for many of us, is so forbiddingly complicated that we often run away from it as fast as we can.

We are totally entranced with the idea of leaving a loving "perfect last impression." This is something that never consciously occurred to us until now. We wholeheartedly agree that love is energy; that it can indeed be shown to our heirs by virtue of our intentions and by expressing our intent through proper handling of our estate. This book makes it evident and unequivocal: we must plan for our demise or risk leaving our loved ones uncomfortable or at odds with one another, not realizing how much we loved, cherished, and appreciated them and cared about their relationships with each other.

Everyone needs this book. Even those who have already planned their estate need to review their plan and consider using the beautiful expressions in this book. We send our love to all who read this book. We fervently pray that they will take its message to heart.

Scott and Shannon Peck
Authors of *The Love You Deserve* and *Liberating Your Magnificence*
Co-Founders of The Love Center

PREFACE

The Perfect Last Impression organizes into one simple concept a multitude of ideas and thoughts gathered from our clients through many years. Simply stated, your estate plan is a *personal* communication between you and your heirs.

Today, most individuals view estate planning as a series of legal documents and decisions that allow them to do three things: save taxes, protect their estate from creditors, and pass the greatest amount of assets on to their heirs. Of course, many professionals in the field of estate planning see helping individuals complete these documents and make these decisions as a lucrative business. Unfortunately, somehow in the midst of it all, the true reason for estate planning has been lost.

We talk to people about these issues on a daily basis. Only rarely do we find someone who has not had a personal negative experience regarding the passing of loved ones and the distribution of the resulting estate. Most often these experiences invoke passionate and highly charged emotions; often these experiences have long lasting and even harmful emotional effects. Clearly, there is something wrong with our current methods of estate planning.

Are we saying then, that legal, tax, and other practical issues should be ignored? Of course not! A good understanding of relevant methods of estate planning should be encouraged. Indeed a good portion of this book is dedicated to exploration of such matters. But we believe that a new dimension needs to be added to the mix in order to fulfill the human needs of love, understanding, and compassion that are so obviously missing from the type of planning being done today.

How is this accomplished? Communication! Most often people never communicate about the planning of their estate with the very people who are most important to its success—their heirs! In fact, in many cases they do not even want their heirs to know what's going on. This reluctance to communicate with the people who will be most deeply affected often stems from fear. Fear on the part of the parents, or the children, of discussing death. Fear, perhaps, of facing an unpleasant reaction regarding the distribution of the property among the heirs. Many other factors play into this fear. In this book, you learn how to overcome these fears and how to open the dialogue for a more successful outcome of estate planning.

The way that you pass your estate on to your heirs will have a profound effect on them. The way you distribute your estate, though it may appear to be only legal documents, actually says volumes to your heirs about your feelings for them and their importance in your life. For this reason *The Perfect Last Impression* was written from the standpoint that an estate plan essentially boils down to a communication, a way of speaking to those left behind.

Why is this communication so important? We have come to realize that what is passed to your heirs is not just money or material possessions. Your estate actually has far more human and emotional value than material possessions, in and of themselves, can possibly convey. This is why more intimate communication, be it written or face-to-face, is crucial in engendering family harmony and understanding. When strife, dissension, and havoc occur in the aftermath of the death of a loved one, it is almost never simply a money issue. More often than not, it is a direct result of emotional distress caused by misunderstanding between the deceased and the heirs.

Almost everyone who is planning his estate desires to be remembered in the best light possible, especially by their loved ones. A good estate plan is the last communication, and, if properly done, will accomplish this goal.

This book is called *The Perfect Last Impression* because that is precisely what it is designed to help you do. Experience is a very powerful teacher. However, it is impossible to learn from your own experience when it comes to transferring your estate to your heirs. Once the time comes to make that transfer, you are no longer around to perform damage control. For your heirs, it is also difficult to recover from the personal trauma if a poorly planned estate causes irreparable damage to family relationships. So it becomes crucial to learn from other people's examples and mistakes.

This book contains a wealth of examples and experiences gleaned from our clients over the years. Actual case studies show how lack of communication about a well-planned estate can wreak havoc upon heirs. We have also provided real-life examples to show how good communication can bring families together.

To help in understanding how we have lost the human touch with our present estate planning methods, we demonstrate historically how we got to where we are today in the estate planning field.

We give you information in very simple and understandable language showing all the different common estate planning tools and how they will, or won't, work for you. We start with the "Do Nothing" plan and move through wills and trusts to the more complicated tools, such as charitable remainder trusts and offshore trusts. And, we demonstrate how these methods can be indirect communications to your heirs all by themselves.

We show you how to get started on your estate plan and how to work with your attorney to achieve the goals you have laid out, to reach a plan that will leave the perfect last impression with your heirs.

We have also given you a great list of DO's and DON'Ts to help you in all facets of your planning.

Please remember that all legal issues involved in your estate planning process should always be discussed with an estate

planning attorney in your state for application to your specific situation. While current and accurate, the information given in this book is not to be construed as legal or financial advice and is not to be relied upon for specific individual estate planning under any circumstance.

We hope that this book will be read and its ideas implemented by all professionals who work in this field—estate planning attorneys, accountants, financial planners, insurance professionals, and all who work with clients on the final disposition of their estates. We have not intended this book to be relied upon as a technical manual on the law of estate planning—far from it. This book is designed to promote communication as part of the art of estate planning, an all-new way of looking at an age-old subject.

The heirs of those who put into practice the ideas in this book can avoid tremendous hardship, heartache, and lasting grief. Even more importantly, great warmth, love, and lasting benefit can be derived from putting these valuable principles into practice. By using what is offered in this book, you will be able not simply to transfer your assets, but to leave your heirs a wonderful, loving final message. The true mission of this book is to show you how to create the perfect last impression. We dedicate it to you, our reader, with the hope that it can help you accomplish all these important goals and promote harmony and love within your family.

INTRODUCTION

Estate planning, as it is commonly done today, needs a drastic makeover.

The process of passing one's earthly belongings to one's heirs—whether that be a spouse, children, another loved one, a charity, or a close acquaintance—is too often viewed as simply a legal, even mechanical, process. However, the process of planning and carrying out an estate transfer is much more than a routine legal matter. An estate plan is, in fact, the final communication and, therefore, perhaps the most significant of all messages that human beings deliver to those they leave behind.

Your estate plan is one of the best opportunities you'll have to communicate your fondest feelings to your heirs. With an estate plan, you can express what has been most important to you in life and leave your heirs with a final message that can greatly impact their lives.

However, based on our extensive experience in observing both those on the giving end and those on the receiving end of an estate transfer, we have seen that miscommunication abounds and often results in dreadful long-term consequences. We were particularly dismayed when we heard about Sally. (All names used in the book have been changed to protect the privacy of the individuals involved. All examples, however, are real.)

Sally's story influenced our decision to write this book, and we share it to illustrate the profound emotional content that lies within what many people view as *only* legal documents. From Sally's story and from countless other similar experiences, it's evident that the process of transferring material assets to one's heirs also delivers spiritual and emotional messages as well.

When Sally was eight years old, her mother died very suddenly. At the time, Sally's two older brothers were serving overseas in the armed forces. Sally's father, who was a wealthy man, remarried Sharon, a woman with two children—a girl who was just seven months older than Sally and a boy who was five years older.

When Sally was in her early 30s, her father died. Since her father had no estate plan in place, according to the laws of the state, everything went to Sally's stepmother, Sharon. Initially, this didn't seem to be a problem. In fact, Sally thought little of it. She had established a close relationship with Sharon through the years, and even though her father was now gone, Sally still saw herself as a full-fledged member of the family.

Sharon eventually remarried and moved away. As time passed, she gradually phased out both of Sally's brothers from her life. Sally didn't like that, but she knew Sharon and her brothers had never been more than cordial to one another anyway. Unlike Sally, her brothers had not been raised by Sharon, as they were adults and already on their own when their father remarried. Sally thought it was natural that she had a stronger bond with her stepmother than her brothers did.

Yet, the relationship between Sally and Sharon began to erode. There were long stretches of time with no contact while Sharon and her new husband traveled. There were periods when Sharon was hospitalized, and Sally was never notified. Sharon ignored Sally's children and didn't call or even send a card for their birthdays. Sally was hurt, but she still tried to maintain the relationship and regain closeness to her stepmother.

Sally sometimes thought her efforts were working but soon discovered some telltale signs to the contrary. Sharon had already given much of the inheritance money to Sally's stepbrother. The stepbrother had also been gifted virtually all of the family heirlooms, such as the china and silver. Then, Sharon gave all of her jewelry (and there was a lot of it) to Sally's stepsister and her stepsister's daughters. Some of this jewelry had belonged to Sally's mother and had been promised to Sally by her father. When Sally discovered she was not even included as a beneficiary of her stepmother's family trust, she was so hurt that she finally broke off the relationship altogether.

"I have never felt so rejected and unloved," said Sally, expressing her emotional turmoil. "It isn't the money. I don't need that. My husband and I do very well, and I have always been self-sufficient. It was the rejection as a member of the family that hurt so much! And, to make matters worse, she wouldn't even talk to me about this." Sally concluded with this telling

xxiv   The Perfect Last Impression

remark: "I know my father would be mortified. Why didn't he love us enough to protect me and my brothers?"

Many people who are left in similar circumstances share Sally's feelings. Interestingly enough, though it was Sharon who actually cut Sally out of the estate, Sally ultimately blames her father for a lack of caring and foresight. Because her father failed to have an estate plan, Sally ended up feeling that he didn't love her enough to protect her interests. Most likely, this was not true at all. Undoubtedly, Sally's father loved his children very much and thought he was doing the right thing by taking care of his wife and trusting her to care for them. Yet they will never know for sure. His lack of communication in this regard meant Sally was left to draw her own conclusions, which resulted in an empty, negative last impression of her father.

Another example shows how disaster can be avoided by anticipating problems and ensuring that proper communication is in place. Recently, two young men, Brad and David, visited Jeanne to discuss the estate of their father, Harold, who was very ill. Harold had prepared a revocable living trust several years earlier. Now hospitalized with a life-threatening illness, he was anxious to make some changes to the trust immediately. He sent Brad and David to Jeanne. David was the appointed successor trustee of the trust, and Harold wanted David to represent him in discussing changes he felt were necessary.

Harold had a modest estate, with his home being the major asset. The home was in a desirable location, and it had greatly appreciated in value over the years. Widowed at a young age,

Harold had raised his three sons (the third son was named Eric) and daughter, Mary, by himself. Strangely enough, the original trust provided that, upon Harold's death, the home was to go to Eric, who would pay a predetermined price for the house by making payments to his three siblings.

However, according to the existing trust, Eric was to pay his siblings their share of the purchase price at very low payments of principal only—no interest—spread over a 20-year period. In reviewing the trust, it was obvious the preset purchase price was less than half of what the property was worth on the current market. In addition, because the payments Eric would make were without interest and spread over such a long period of time, it meant his brothers and sister would actually receive very little from the house. This was patently unfair since there was no other property in the estate to balance the distribution. One child out of the four was going to receive almost the entire inheritance.

When Jeanne asked why Harold had decided to distribute the estate in this manner, David said he wasn't sure. He believed it was because Eric had lived with their father for years after the others had moved away. However, things had recently changed. Eric had married and moved out of the house, and Mary, now divorced with children, had moved in.

Now Harold wanted to give the house to Mary. As Jeanne met with David and Brad, she could see the brothers were clearly uncomfortable with their father's existing estate plan, but she sensed they didn't feel the suggested changes were any better.

The two brothers didn't feel they were being treated equally but didn't know how to communicate their dissatisfaction to Harold without appearing greedy or disrespectful.

Additionally, David realized that, as trustee, he would be tasked with distributing the payments on the house from Mary to his brothers for a period of 20 years. David confided to Jeanne that he did not want to act as trustee at all.

The three decided that Jeanne should meet with Harold to discuss some of these issues. When they met, Harold was resistant to any change in his plans. He insisted that Jeanne transfer the house to Mary; he also stipulated that the amount she be required to pay her brothers be cut in half. Now things were twice as unfair.

Harold explained to Jeanne that, as a divorced mother of three children, Mary couldn't afford to pay more than that. He admitted to Jeanne that he wanted all of his children to own a home and that, at present, only one of them did. Still, he told Jeanne that he had explained to his children his reasons for changing the trust and they had approved.

Jeanne spoke to Harold at length, mentioning that, at the very least, David and Brad did not feel the plan was fair. Jeanne told Harold that children often will not express their true feelings about these matters directly to their parents or other family members; she explained that children do not want to seem greedy, disrespectful or disloyal. Harold saw that perhaps he was mistaken in thinking it was right to make the changes he had suggested. He said he loved all of his children equally and didn't want to hurt any of them. He really thought he was doing the right thing by keeping the house in the family but decided to rethink his decision and consider any alternative plans that might come to light.

At Jeanne's suggestion, David got his siblings together to discuss this matter. At their meeting, they came up with a plan that would be fair to all four of them and would provide a means for each to buy a house. The plan was simply to sell their father's home at market value and share the proceeds. After the meeting, David felt comfortable in presenting the plan to his father personally since he now felt that, instead of being greedy, he was actually speaking for the best interests of all the children. In addition, David told his father that he did not want to serve as the successor trustee, but that his sister did. The father agreed, and the changes his children suggested were made to his trust.

In this case, because Harold listened and communicated while there was still time, he was able to create a final communication that left a much more loving message than his original estate plan. Initially Harold thought by leaving the house to one of his children, he was keeping his most prized possession in the family and, thus, was leaving a part of himself behind. This may be important. However, in this case, what Harold saw as a way of leaving something of himself behind actually left an inappropriate message because his original plan benefited only one of the children and was unfair to the rest. By equalizing the distribution of his assets, the father was in effect spreading his love, approval, and respect to all four of his children—which was really his intent in the first place.

Harold's children later told Jeanne that once they opened up and expressed their feelings about their father's plans, they realized there was a lot more than money involved. It wasn't the house or the money that concerned them the most but rather what the estate plan represented as an expression of their father's love. For each of the children, the way the trust was structured was a statement of their father's approval or non-approval. Mary was to be rewarded more than her brothers simply because she had been the one to move in with their father. The three sons felt they were being punished for reasons that were unclear. In effect, they felt that their father, whom they obviously loved and respected, was being unjust and unloving in his distribution. These feelings were deep and very strong, and they realized, subconsciously, that Harold's estate plan was wrong. They knew it spelled disaster and would lead to problems in the family.

This story illustrates a fairly common scenario. Often, when it comes to estate planning, parents cannot honestly communicate with their children about the subject and children cannot honestly express their feelings to their parents. All too often fear gets in the way. Children fear that they will appear greedy, ungrateful, or disloyal; parents fear discussing death and their true feelings about it with their children. As is often the case, David and his siblings needed a third-party professional to facilitate communication and bring out the underlying emotional content of the estate transfer. Once Harold was able to communicate his true feelings and the children were able to respond with their ideas, an estate plan that communicated on an intimate level was accomplished.

The critically important point is this: An estate plan is a *personal*, lasting, highly important way of communicating with one's heirs. Too often, as in the case of Sally and her father, individuals don't seize the opportunity to put a perfect final communication in place. They typically end up creating a plan that is nothing more than an economic transfer of material assets. The loving message a properly structured estate plan could have delivered is sadly lost.

In our many years of observing the individual reactions and responses of countless heirs, we have concluded that <u>estate transfer is communication of the most intimate kind</u>. Much more than a transfer and distribution of worldly goods, estate planning is a process that has a profound emotional and spiritual effect. Yet most people don't approach estate planning with the thought that they are formulating their final message to the world and, especially, to their heirs.

Much can be gained with the simple shift in understanding and realization that plans for transferring an estate have a more important underlying purpose—communicating with one's heirs. For your estate plan to communicate the message you would like, you need not only a new awareness but also understanding of an entirely different language than is traditional in estate planning. This book provides useful information that will guide you in making decisions about the legal aspects of your estate transfer. However, more importantly, you will gain new insights about the purpose of an estate plan and the tools needed to structure a final communication that says exactly what you want to convey.

We strongly believe that this transfer process_and the planning necessary to accomplish it_is the deepest, most lasting communication human beings may ever have with those they leave behind. How this transition is handled equates to a statement of love, respect, and honor for both the giver and the receiver. When loving thought is left out of estate planning, a lifetime of family strife can be the result.

Remember, communication between all parties involved is usually the primary key for promoting long-lasting harmony. That is why this book encourages communication and explains how communication and good estate planning can minimize strife and conflict within the family. It examines various common methods used in such planning, revealing the merits and demerits of each in terms of their ability to help accomplish the primary purpose—that of good communication with the heirs.

We have not meant this book to be a legal treatise on the intricacies of estate plans. Therefore, specific solutions to situations within your particular plan should always to be discussed and resolved with your estate planning attorney. However, this book will be a useful resource in helping with that communication.

More than anything, this book is about adding a new dimension to your estate plan. We strongly urge and encourage each of you—either on your own or in working with a professional team of lawyers and accountants—to use these ideas to formulate an estate plan that expresses your true feelings.

FIRST AND LAST IMPRESSIONS

First impressions are so important that many people expend exorbitant amounts of time and attention worrying about making the perfect first impression. However, <u>in terms of significance and enduring impact, the first impression pales in comparison to the last impression</u>. Yet, many of us ignore the last chance, the best chance of all, to communicate a loving last impression to those who are most important to us.

Consider the work and worry that many people put into making sure initial encounters are just right. Most good salespeople go to great lengths to make sure they come off as professional as possible the first time they meet a potential customer. Then, to keep that good first impression alive, some even keep meticulous records just to make sure that when they call on their customer again, they don't wear the same outfit they wore the time before.

Business consultants, vendors, and service providers may be concerned with the impression that their car might make on a potential client. One businessman ultimately sold his expensive sports car because he was afraid it might give potential clients the impression that he was irresponsible and careless. Initially, he parked two blocks away from his meetings so his customers wouldn't see the car. When he tired of this inconvenience, he bought a new car more appropriate to the image he wanted to project. Now he purposely has customers join him as he walks out to his expensive, but conservative, car. He does everything he possibly can to make a great first impression. And his efforts pay off.

Successful job applicants also know the importance of first impressions. They take great care with their appearance, making sure they are dressed appropriately for their interview. They research the company. They know the major players, their backgrounds, and their current position in the company. They may even take a job with a competitor to learn the business before they make a stab at working for the company with whom they really want to build their career.

Think about the time and effort put into making a good impression on a first date. New clothes, hair styling, bathing, perfuming, nail care, breath mints, and deodorants. Madison Avenue makes a fortune pandering products that promise a successful impression for this one event!

Whether it's in the interest of building a client base, getting a job, or impressing a date, why do we go to all this trouble and expense for an initial encounter? Obviously, most people realize that a bad first impression is hard to overcome. It takes a lot to change a person's mind about us once an impression has been formed.

It's been suggested that making a poor first impression can be compared to losing money in the stock market. Why? It's because, in regards to both investments and impressions, it's so much tougher to come back from a loss. In the world of investments, if you suffer an initial loss, it's not just a matter of gaining the money back again. The investor has less to work with and thus has to take greater risk just to recover. For example, it requires a 33-percent gain to make up for an initial 25-percent loss. On the other hand, if you realize an initial gain from your investment, it's much easier to build on that gain.

Similarly, if we bungle a first impression, we may be able to eventually establish our credibility, but it takes more work to regain lost ground. Obviously, a poor first impression can have serious negative results. We may not get the job or secure a second date. We may lose a sale or fail to meet our quotas.

Granted, the results of making a poor first impression can be quite unfortunate and unpleasant. Yet, in every case, we can recover. We can learn from the experience, make corrections, and try again. However, this is not the case when it comes to last impressions.

In terms of significance and enduring impact, first impressions pale in comparison to last impressions. While a poor first impression may have serious negative results, imagine the dire consequences of leaving a poor last impression. If we create a poor last impression, we are stuck with it for eternity!

Even so, not much is said about the last impression. What do we mean by a last impression anyway? In this instance we are referring to the final communication people leave upon their death. We can't learn from the way we leave this message and change it next time—because there isn't going to be a next time. That's the whole point. This final communication is not only the last impression; it's the lasting impression because it can't be changed. What could be more important than leaving a final, permanent, loving last impressionable gift of ourselves for the people we love the most?

Although most people give this little or no thought, <u>the last impression may be the most critical communication of our entire lifetime</u>. Much of our striving to lead good lives and to be successful in the eyes of our community is dedicated to the idea of being a good example and leaving a great impression. Yet many of us fail to take advantage of the best chance of all to communicate a loving last impression to those who are most important to us.

These last impressions can be critical. One of our closest friends, Robert, had an experience that illustrates how absolutely important this communication can be. He and his wife had a major disagreement one night. When they went to bed they were still angry with each other. The next morning, Robert discovered that his wife, a woman in her early 40s, had died in her sleep of a heart attack. He was so emotionally distraught by her death and by the fact that he did not have a chance to tell her he really did love her—and to hear reassurances that she really did love him—that it took him more than five years to deal with her passing.

It may seem as though this couple had no opportunity to leave a last impression. Neither Robert nor his wife had any reason to believe she would die in her sleep. What, if anything, could have been done to help this situation?

What if this couple had organized an estate plan specifically designed to leave a loving, caring final message for each other? Would that have helped Robert? Most likely it would have. If there had been some word from her letting him know she loved and respected him, no matter what state of mind she might have been in at the time of her death, it might have helped him move on much sooner.

Do you know the last time that you will ever work on an important business project with someone, entertain a certain acquaintance in your home, talk to a loved one, or have dinner with a friend? The answer, of course, is No. Death is maddeningly unpredictable. You have no way of knowing when an event, a conversation, or a meeting will prove to be the last.

Does that mean you have no way to control the last impression? Yes, to a great extent, it means exactly that. Fortunately, when it comes to leaving an impression on the people nearest and dearest to your heart, there is a major exception to the rule.

A client came into Jeanne's office recently with a very simple but very touching request. He wanted to include a poem in his trust so his children could read how he truly felt about them. Jeanne asked if he had written the poem himself. He hadn't but had found one that perfectly expressed how he felt about his son and daughter. He said he wanted to be able to look down from wherever he was and see that his children were happy and that they knew he had really loved them. He wanted the poem included in the trust, but he didn't know where to put it. It was decided to make a place for it in his trust portfolio.

By including the poem, this man was ensuring that he would leave a loving, caring, and lasting communication with his heirs. His children will treasure this communication for the rest of their lives, not only because of the words of the poem, but because of their father's kind action to have it included in his trust. This last impression will help this man's children know him a little better. It may also help them deal with his death and soften the loss. His final communication will most likely help his children feel more love toward one another and bring them closer together as well. Perhaps it will even motivate them to plan the same type of communication for their children.

Over the years, children of our clients have sometimes expressed great disappointment in the way their parents' estate was passed on to them. The complaint isn't that they didn't get the things they expected. Usually, they felt the property distribution worked out fine. Often the children were wealthier than their parents had been, and they didn't care too much about the money they had received. What was painfully missing, however, was any final word, any last expression of love or caring. In most of these cases, there was a last impression, but it was delivered by an attorney. It was cold, unfeeling, legal, and barren of what the children really wanted. They would have much rather heard a tender thought, a reminder that one of their achievements had made their parents proud, or even a funny inside joke.

At times, parents use their estate plan as a way to even an imagined score—leaving an unequal distribution to their children or skipping a child altogether because they think they have already provided enough for that child during their lifetimes. In other cases, parents put various restrictions on a child's inheritance because they perceive that child as unable to handle his or her own affairs, perhaps because of drug use, alcoholism, or some other reason.

These decisions often make sense, logically and legally, but what is forgotten is that these acts deal with deeply emotional and private family matters. When the decisions are made arbitrarily and delivered without explanation and in cold, unfeeling language, they can leave deep scars on those left behind. In addition, they can promote unnecessary jealousy, hate, animosity, and resentment, all of which can result in permanent rifts among family members.

The negative implications of one-sided or restrictive plans can be avoided with proper communication. In the following chapters, we will explore the prevalent ways estate plans are created and provide examples and sample language that can serve to alleviate negative last impressions.

While a good first impression may be important in sales and dating, we recommend that you take what we call the "actor's" approach in life. Most actors and actresses know that a grand exit is one of the most important parts of a play. The exit is the last thing the audience sees and is probably the thing the audience will remember most. A weak ending ruins a play, just as a weak exit may ruin much of the good you have tried to do in life. Why not plan a grand exit, so that when you leave this life, you leave a perfect impression on those you love—an impression that they will remember fondly forever.

CHAPTER 2

PLANNING AHEAD

All too frequently people fail to plan for their death. We have witnessed these consequences firsthand. What follows_Carl's story_demonstrates an example of what can happen when someone fails to plan.

Carl's mother's last communication was not well executed. Her last impression left a message that was unfavorable and emotionally damaging to her children and their relationship with one another.

Carl was quite busy with his small dental practice. A fairly happy guy, Carl loved to tell jokes, and his patients enjoyed being around him. He did have a problem with his mother, Darla, however. Darla was what Carl privately called "a piece of work." She was self-involved, demanding, and unappreciative. On top of that, she was a hypochondriac, and her constant worries about health—along with her feelings of abandonment and martyrdom—were enough to drive away Carl very quickly, even when his infrequent visits did occur.

Carl's sister, Helen, lived in the same small city as their mother. Helen was divorced, her children were grown, and she had the time and the patience to take care of Darla. Carl and Helen were fairly close, and Helen kept her brother informed of their mother's ongoing episodes. Helen was not financially well off, so Carl often sent her small amounts of money. He presumed that Helen used the money for her own needs and those of their mother. He thought this was the least he could do in lieu of not being able to visit more often.

Once, when Darla came down with an actual illness, Carl paid a visit and saw firsthand the toll the constant caretaking was having on Helen. In a moment of generosity mixed with guilt, Carl told Darla—in Helen's presence—that even though Mom had considerable assets, she should leave everything to Helen as payment for her services.

When Darla died several months later, her heirs found that she had done exactly as Carl had suggested in his moment of over-exuberant generosity. Helen received everything, and Carl got absolutely nothing.

Carl was emotionally devastated. He never thought his mother would act on his suggestion and disinherit him. He felt unloved, rejected, and resentful. His sister's attitude was just as surprising. She seemed to feel that if Carl didn't mean it, he shouldn't have said it. Besides, she believed she had earned the estate, so she was going to keep it. Carl felt betrayed by both his sister and his mother, and the poorly planned estate transfer ruined the relationship Carl and Helen once had. They haven't been close since Darla died.

What happened here? A lack of forethought and lopsided communication was combined with faulty reasoning and inconsiderate planning. Carl did not communicate his full intentions to his mother and his sister. His seemingly noble gesture was motivated by guilt and a desire to acknowledge his sister's efforts. He expected his mother and sister to discern his true feelings. In spite of what he said, he hoped they would think of his best interests. Yet Carl's mother and sister took what he said literally. Helen didn't acknowledge the fact that Carl deserved better and that he had often helped with their mother. She considered only her own sacrifices and reward.

If Darla had thought things through, she probably would have realized that Carl should have a portion of her inheritance and that he would be hurt by being disinherited. Perhaps she was just not well enough to care, or maybe she was unduly influenced by Helen. She may have wanted to punish Carl for not being there or maybe she even felt that she was showing her love by honoring Carl's spoken request. Carl will never know.

Unfortunately, these situations are all too common. <u>Often, when it comes time to make decisions about the disposition of our estates, no real communication takes place</u> between all parties that will be affected. This may be because talking about dying is painful and frightening for most of us. When thinking about our own death or the death of a loved one, we often recoil. We may become fearful, think irrationally, or withdraw into ourselves, and we may consider our own wants ahead of the needs of others.

Carl's mother's last communication was shortsighted. She considered what Helen had done for her most recently but failed to think back over the many things Carl had done. She also failed to look to the future and the ongoing effects her actions would have on her children. Had she really thought about it, Darla would most likely have wanted her final communication to produce different results.

Estate planning often treads a delicate emotional balance beam. There are so many situations in which a thoughtful approach, along with a full and loving explanation of the decisions, can make a crucial difference. Many, if not most, attorneys who practice in this area are not trained to think about the emotional side of the equation. They are not psychologists or therapists. They often don't inquire as to the reasons behind their clients' requests.

In a way, attorneys are simply technicians. They precisely translate the wishes of the client into the proper legal terms, leaving no ambiguity as to what should occur in terms of the legal and financial transfer of the estate. This is a difficult and exacting job, because the legal ramifications of certain terminology can put the client in a position they never imagined. The threat of lawsuits also plagues attorneys, so they focus on making their actions as legally correct as possible.

Given this, you can see why attorneys typically cannot, or will not, suggest that an estate plan address the emotional needs of the heirs. Their training teaches them that looking on the emotional side of estate planning is not part of their job, or perhaps they feel that such a suggestion is an infringement on a client's personal relationships.

In most cases, attorneys are not going to be the ones to suggest that their clients take a different approach. Change has to come from the client. In order to ensure that estate planning becomes a more personal, thoughtful, and positive process, clients must insist that their emotional and spiritual priorities show up in the disposition of their estates.

We have felt a real urgency to encourage more people to push for this kind of change in estate planning. Perhaps the catalyst that prompts us is our background in estate planning combined with knowledge of what lies ahead.

We are about to embark on the nation's largest intergenerational transfer of wealth. Over the next ten years or so, approximately $6 trillion will change hands through inheritances in the United States alone. This is by far the largest amount of money that will ever be transferred between generations. The Baby Boomers, most of whom have parents now in their 60s and 70s, will be the recipients of this transfer of wealth. That is all well and good, except for the one undeniable fact that all this inherited money can be the stimulus for division in families.

We already have the most fractured society with the most alienated children and the most disrupted families in the history of the world. We already have too many people who measure their self-worth—and absolutely everything else, for that matter—in terms of money; too many people who, too often, use money for control, manipulation, and punishment. We already have a large portion of society in which the pursuit of money comes first, the protection of material things comes second, and the concern and care for others comes last. This nightmare will only intensify as a huge wave of cash, with all its potential for destruction of family bonds and emotional ties, is added to the picture.

As an estate owner, you are in a position to change this nightmarish picture within your own family. Though it may take a little work, you can use your estate plan to help bring your family together, rather than have them torn apart over pieces of paper and other merely tangible goods. If we have learned anything from our own lives and from watching hundreds of others affected by the transfer of an estate, it is that in the end, it is not money that counts. When we are on our deathbeds, we are probably not going to be thinking about how we could have invested in Microsoft when it was only $12 a share. We are not going to be wishing for another few moments so we can call the bank and transfer that $9,000 into a CD we have been waiting to open.

We don't deny money is important. However, it is not all-important. In fact, from what we have seen, money's primary importance comes from the fact that it serves as a measuring stick that reveals how we feel for others. Mary's story illustrates how the resolution of an estate can be this kind of an emotional measuring stick.

Mary had two brothers. Their mother, Fran, was deceased. Fran was divorced when the children were small, but she had married Nathan and lived with him for many years before her death. Nathan had one daughter, Michelle, from a prior marriage. Michelle, Mary, and the two boys always got along well, and they were a very happy family. Fran and Nathan had a trust, which directed that half of the estate would go to Michelle and the other half would be divided among Mary and her two brothers. That was fine.

However, after Fran's death, Nathan removed almost half the assets from the trust and placed them in his and Michelle's names. When he passed away, Michelle wanted half of the assets remaining in the original trust, which is what the trust document dictated. Mary didn't know what to do. Her brothers were upset with Michelle, and Mary was concerned that the family would be split apart.

Mary called an attorney, who set up a conference call with Michelle and Mary. During the call, the attorney explained possible solutions to the problem. One solution would be to have the problem resolved in a court of law. This would be expensive and would waste a goodly portion of the estate. The attorney also indicated that, if this matter was taken to court, the judge would most likely abide by what the parents' intentions had been when they originally drew up the trust. The attorney felt a judge would order that the assets that had been removed from the trust and given to Michelle would have to be restored before any distribution of the trust took place.

After more discussion, both Mary and Michelle agreed that pursuing litigation was not worth taking the chance of destroying the relationship that existed among the four children. Michelle apologized to Mary, saying she did not understand how the trust was supposed to work. Michelle thought her father was free to do whatever he wanted with the estate before his death. She thought the assets that were left after he was gone would then be divided as stated in the trust.

However, once the attorney explained that a judge would most likely view it differently and would regard the original intent, Michelle agreed that the estate should include everything that had been transferred to her name by her father.

This is one example that should be celebrated and put up in bright lights for the world to take note. These people all wanted to be fair and loving, but there had been a genuine misunderstanding over the meaning and the terms of the trust. Fortunately for all concerned, their hearts and their priorities were in the right place.

We encourage every individual involved in the important process of estate planning to take responsibility for more positive outcomes. Professional estate planners must take responsibility for throwing light into corners previously overlaid with legalese and shadowed in a reluctance to deal with emotional matters. Estate owners must take responsibility to properly plan for their own death and the transfer of their estate, and heirs must decide to communicate openly and thoroughly about what they would like to see happen in the transfer. It takes a measure of courage and true caring about our families to communicate honestly with them on this level. If you will choose to illuminate your estate planning with the bright light of truth, humility, and love, you can ensure that the nightmares will fade, at least for your own heirs.

CHAPTER 3

THE PURPOSE OF ESTATE PLANNING

Why do people plan for their death and the disbursement of their estate? Is it to save taxes? Is it to avoid probate? Is it to have control over who gets their property and when and how they get it? Or is it an unconscious effort to leave something of themselves when they are gone? Estate planning is a combination of all of these things, and it is also something more. Perhaps the most compelling reason people plan to transfer their estate is that they want to express their love, care, and concern for their families and other loved ones. They want to be remembered with love and respect in return.

Who among us doesn't want those left behind to entertain fond memories of us when we are gone? We have yet to hear anyone tell us that the object of his estate planning was to incite hatred and cause alienation among his heirs. While poor planning often causes these negative results, the person's intention is not usually to hurt or harm his loved ones.

Rather than an attempt to divide the family and cause discord, estate planning is primarily viewed as a way to express love and goodwill to a person's heirs and to communicate these fond feelings through the distribution of worldly belongings. <u>Transferring an estate is a way to share a piece of ourselves and demonstrate our fondest emotions</u>. This is exactly how the heirs interpret it even though their predecessor's feelings are ultimately translated into monetary terms. Therefore, this transfer must be handled judiciously, so that a wrong or false impression isn't communicated. <u>The old adage "It's not what you say that counts, it's how you say it!" certainly holds true in estate planning</u>. Planning for transferring your estate at the time of your death is simply a way of saying "I love you" to your loved ones. The fact that such a plan is also a gift of money and assets is only a valuable side benefit.

While we have established the fact that a heartfelt expression to your heirs is the primary motivation for estate planning, other motivating factors need to be explored as well. Avoiding probate, saving taxes, and protecting assets are also important reasons for taking a close look at the intricacies of your estate plan. Interestingly, these secondary factors are also essentially a way to express caring, since they determine the shape and character of the plan and dictate its ultimate effectiveness and its overall benefit to the heirs. It's important to note that some of these objectives could be in conflict with others. For instance, the tools used to save taxes are often different from the ones used for asset protection, and one benefit may need to be sacrificed to achieve the other. So it's often necessary at the outset to determine whether asset protection is more important than saving taxes, or vice versa.

As we discuss the various choices and alternatives that go into building an effective estate plan, it's important to understand that this process is often made up of three very distinct phases. The first phase entails identifying the objectives and assessing the options. Often, this phase includes face-to-face counseling with a professional who understands all the alternatives. Such an individual will ask the person creating the estate plan a number of questions. These questions will help determine that particular person's situation and pinpoint the person's goals. An individual who is creating an estate plan should spend the time necessary in this phase, and should, in most cases, use the services of a professional in order to gain an understanding of all the legal facets involved in any proposed plan.

In the second phase, the documents are actually drafted.

The third phase is a thorough explanation of the ongoing responsibilities of all parties involved, including the estate planning client, the heirs, and any professionals who may be involved. The depth of this entire process will depend upon the type of plan being used as well as the size of the estate.

However, before we become too involved with the actual process of estate planning, it is wise to remember that there have been two great themes or trends that have long been prominent in the passing of estates. The first theme is what we call the leaving of "value" to our heirs: the passing on of family trends, beliefs, traditions, attitudes, and strategies for successful living. The second theme relates to the legal "ownership" of estate property. We believe that the modern approach to estate planning has placed inordinate attention on the theme of owner-ship, to the point of detriment to the heirs, and even to the point of destruction of family relationships.

In order to understand how and why this has taken place, let's take a minute to give you a brief overview of the development of the law with respect to the passage of personal possessions and to the passing of rights to the use and ownership of the land. While we are not going to attempt to explain every detail of the long and complicated history regarding these themes, a few highlights might be useful.

The great underlying principles of our current inheritance laws are derived from English common law. The Norman Conquest in 1066 brought the age of feudalism in England, an age in which the king owned all the land under his control. He allowed his nobles the use of the land with the provision that they were to raise armies from among their peasants or, at mini-mum, to make financial contributions for that purpose. This right of usage was passed automatically to the noble's eldest liv-ing male heir, a practice called "primogeniture." The land was not willed. The only question was the identity of the eldest male heir. This system tended to concentrate all wealth in the hands of a very few people. The English feudal system did recognize wills, but either the king or the Church administered these wills, and the wills did not transfer land—only personal prop-erty. There was constant conflict between the king and the Church over the right to carry out this duty and to collect the associated administrative fees.

It wasn't until 1540, when Parliament passed the Statute of Wills, that title to real property could be willed to one's heirs in England. In the meantime, two types of titles had been developed. The legal titleholder was the person who owned the land, and the beneficial titleholder was the person with the right to the use and benefits of the land. This was the very beginning of the law of trusts. As the laws developed, the government acquired the right to tax property at the time of the owner's death. The Stamp Act, which passed in the late 1700s, made this government right official, stating a certain type of paper printed by the government had to be used to pass an estate. These papers had certain stamps—official government seals of approval—depending on the size of the estate. When an estate was passed on, the court would check the size of the estate against the stamps affixed to the legal documents in order to ensure the proper amount of tax was paid. The court would also check to see whether any gifts had been made in contemplation of death. These gifts were assumed to be transfers at death, and so they were taxed as well. Thus, the first gift tax was instigated.

In the United States, the first estate tax was passed in 1797 to pay for the costs of the Revolutionary War. This tax was repealed in 1802. Another was passed in 1862 to raise revenue to pay for the Civil War. This second estate tax was repealed eight years later, in 1870. Twenty-eight years later, the Spanish War tax was passed. This was a tax on personal property that was passed by will and was unrelated to real estate. The Spanish War tax was not repealed until 1902. In 1916, a federal estate tax, called the German War tax, was passed; this tax is still on the books today. The constitutionality of this tax was supported by Article I, Section 8, which states in part: "Congress shall have Power to lay and collect Taxes, Duties, Imposts and Excises, to pay Debts and provide for the common Defence and general Welfare of the United States; but all Duties, Imposts and Excises shall be uniform throughout the United States" [sic].

The German War tax was not a tax directly on property. It was, and is, a tax on the transfer of the property from deceased people to their heirs. Consequently, it fit within the meaning of the constitutional provision cited above. Today, we have extensive laws relating to the passing of an estate from one generation to the next. We have estate tax, which is a tax on an estate prior to the transfer of property; inheritance tax, which is a tax on the recipient of the property; and gift tax, which is a tax the giver pays based on the value of the gift. These laws have become so important in various types of estate planning that some people have focused on them, as though avoiding taxes was the sole reason for establishing an estate plan.

In this book, we do not concentrate much on the intricacies of the law and its effect on an estate. That important information is available in other books and from your estate planning attorney. Instead, as we mentioned previously, our discussion in this book addresses what the transfer of your property signifies as a communication between you and your heirs. It seems to us that, in the history of humanity's dealings with the vast subject of inheritance, two dominant themes have emerged. One is the theme of leaving a societal memory, a heritage, or code of conduct for successful living—passing to our children the lessons garnered through generations of hard experience. We call this the leaving of "value" to our heirs, communicating to them the most important things we know.

The second theme is related to ownership, to possessions, and to the means of acquiring both the necessities and the pleasurable things of life. This latter theme has been fully developed in laws relating to the passing of estates. A complete, specialized class of legal professionals (known as estate planning attorneys) has emerged to help people through the maze of these laws. Indeed, in addition to lawyers, many other professionals—including insurance agents, accountants, financial planners, stockbrokers, investment advisors, fiduciaries, trust companies, bankers, and litigation attorneys—touch on this area as well.

While the entire process of estate planning has become formalized and systematic, the end result of such planning has not always been peace and harmony. However, we feel a new trend is developing, one that seems to have come full circle since ancient times, before the concentration on possessions became so intense.

People today want to pass value to their heirs. Will this trend lead to more peace and harmony among families? We devoutly hope so, and we certainly pray we can help promote that result.

CHAPTER 4

THE TAX MAN COMETH

In this chapter, our discussion will be about saving taxes, an area of concern to most people. We have purposely started with a discussion of taxes, not because it's the most important motivating factor behind estate planning, but because it's the most common reason people create an estate plan. Tax considerations are present in all facets of estate planning. Therefore, a brief discussion and explanation about some common tax issues are appropriate.

The types of tax to be considered in estate planning include inheritance taxes, estate taxes, gift taxes, capital gains taxes and, in certain cases, income taxes.

Inheritance Taxes

An inheritance tax is similar to an estate tax. However, while estate taxes are paid by the estate before the transfer to the heirs, inheritance taxes are paid by the person receiving the inheritance. The amount of the inheritance tax is usually based on the closeness of the relationship to the deceased.

Estate Taxes

Federal estate taxes come into play when a person's net estate reaches a certain amount, which is $2,000,000 at the time of this writing. In other words, if an individual dies with a net estate of less than $2,000,000, the estate may not be assessed an estate tax. On the other hand, when an individual dies whose net estate is over the present maximum, an estate tax may be incurred. President Ronald Reagan's administration brought about the current law. In the early '80s, before the law was changed, the estate tax exclusion was only $250,000, and was so complicated that almost no one understood how to use it. The tax exclusion amount is called a "lifetime exemption," meaning estates under the amount specified by law are exempt from federal estate tax. Under the current law, this lifetime exemption is being increased every year and will reach a maximum of $3,500,000 per individual in 2009. Many people, including ill-informed advisors, interpret this to mean that unless the estate is so large that it would be charged an estate tax, there isn't enough property in the estate to be concerned with estate planning. Nothing could be further from the truth!

FEDERAL ESTATE TAX EXEMPTIONS

UNDER CURRENT LAW (YEAR 2007)

YEAR	EXEMPTION AMOUNT PER PERSON
1998	$ 625,000
1999	$ 650,000
2000	$ 675,000
2001	$ 675,000
2002	$ 1,000,000
2003	$ 1,000,000
2004	$ 1,500,000
2005	$ 1,500,000
2006	$ 2,000,000
2007	$ 2,000,000
2008	$ 2,000,000
2009	$ 3,500,000

Any estate that owns stock and bonds or real property needs planning for many reasons other than simply to avoid taxes. These reasons will be discussed in detail in later chapters. Please don't ignore your plan simply because someone gives you this type of mis-information. If your estate's value is under the $2,000,000 lifetime exemption, it simply means your heirs will not have to pay a federal estate tax when they receive the property. That's the good news. The bad news is that <u>if you ignore your opportunity to plan, your heirs will end up paying a lot of other unnecessary costs and expenses</u>. Probate, the most critical of these concerns, will be discussed in detail later.

For those whose estate exceeds the lifetime exemption figure, additional planning is necessary to minimize or eliminate the estate taxes that may apply. The exemption may be used in two ways. During your lifetime, it can be used as a credit against gift tax, or, at your death, the exemption can be applied as a credit against estate tax. The rate for gift taxes and estate taxes is identical due to legislation in the early '80s. This takes some of the benefit out of the large exclusion, since prior to this law an additional and separate gift tax was available. In some cases, the entire exemption is used to make gifts during a person's lifetime. However, using a portion of the exemption means only the amount not used for gifts will be left to cover any later estate tax liabilities that might be incurred at the time of death.

In addition to the lifetime exemption, there is another tax exemption. Each individual may currently gift $12,000 each year to as many people as he/she wishes. The gift tax exemption also changes over time. But whatever the current amount, you, as an estate owner, can gift to each of your children, grandchildren, or other friends and relatives a sum ($12,000 at this writing) each year without paying a gift tax. This is an excellent way to move property out of a large taxable estate on a consistent basis. For example, a couple with a married son who has three children could transfer $1.2 million, tax free, to their son's family over a 10-year period. These gifts would also be tax free to the recipients.

Here is how it could work. Max and Elaine have a large and taxable estate and were advised by their tax planning team that they should begin a maximum gifting program to their children in order to reduce their estate for tax purposes. They were told that they could each give $12,000 to as many people every year as they desired. Their heirs are their son, his wife, and three grandchildren. If, each year, Max and Elaine together give $24,000 to their son, $24,000 to his wife, and $24,000 to each of the grandchildren, it would total $120,000 per year. In 10 years, they will have given away $1,200,000 tax free.

In addition to the two tax benefits of the lifetime exemption and the gift tax exemption discussed above, married couples enjoy another exemption, which allows them to make lifetime unlimited gifts to each another. They may also inherit unlimited amounts from each other tax free. This exemption, called the "Unlimited Marital Deduction," is specifically designed to allow a surviving spouse the ability to enjoy all benefits of the couple's estate. This deduction defers any estate tax until the surviving spouse passes away. If used properly in the estate plan, this deduction, along with the lifetime exemption of the deceased spouse, can save the heirs of a married couple literally hundreds of thousands of dollars in taxes, even on an estate up to two times the current lifetime exemption. (Currently, this would apply to estates valued at $4,000,000 or two times the individual lifetime exemption of $2,000,000.) A more thorough discussion of these tax savings is presented in the chapter on revocable living trusts.

If a federal estate tax is due, it is charged on the amount over and above any remaining lifetime exemption. Currently, the beginning tax rate is 20 percent and extends upward to 45 percent. In some limited cases, the estate tax can be an even greater percentage of the estate. This is an expensive tax. It's easy to see why people would be eager to mitigate it as much as possible.

What about state inheritance taxes? Most states do not have a direct inheritance tax or an estate tax. Instead, many states, including California, Arizona, and Texas, share in a portion of the tax collected by the federal government. Washington, D.C., also receives a share of the federal estate taxes collected from its residents. A few states, including New York and Massachusetts, receive their share of the federal estate tax and collect an additional "estate tax" as well. Then, some states such as North Carolina and Pennsylvania collect an "inheritance tax," which is calculated based on the relationship between the heir and the person who died. Less tax is charged for closer relatives and more for more distant relatives. Again, this inheritance tax is in addition to the state's share of the federal estate tax. Additional information about current practices within your state can be obtained from your estate planning attorney.

Gift Taxes and Capital Gains Taxes

When property is transferred by either sale or gift, one of two kinds of taxes must always be considered. The first is the gift tax, and the second is the capital gains tax. As used in this context, a gift tax is a tax charged by the IRS to the giver of any property that exceeds $12,000 in any one year. The gift is valued at its fair market value at the time the gift is made, and the tax is calculated on this amount. The capital gains tax is taxed to the person who owns the property when it is sold and in its simplest terms is calculated by subtracting the amount originally paid for the property from the sale price of the property.

If a person transfers all, or a portion, of a property by placing anyone other than a spouse on a deed to real property or on the title to a stock certificate or bank account, tax considerations apply. The most common situation in which this occurs is when a parent includes a child as a joint tenant on the title to real estate or stock. Adding the child as a joint tenant makes the child the owner of one-half of such property. However, since the child pays no money for this privilege of ownership, the property is essentially a gift. At some point, this gift will have to be accounted for and taxed. If the estate is small enough, the lifetime exemption may cover the gift(s) made during the giver's lifetime, as well as the balance of the estate being transferred upon the giver's death. If this is the case, no additional tax will be due. However, if the estate is larger, this gift amount will be deducted from the lifetime exemption, and a smaller amount will be available to credit against the estate tax at the time of death.

For example, Alice has an estate of $1,500,000. Her home accounts for $1,000,000 of that amount. In order to avoid probate, Alice places her son, Aaron, on the title to her home as joint tenant with her. By so doing, Alice has given Aaron a gift of $500,000. According to the current limit, Alice now has $1,500,000 left as a lifetime exemption. When she dies, she has $1,000,000 left in her estate. In this scenario, no tax would be due.

However, if Alice has an estate of $2,500,000 and her house is valued at $1,000,000, the story is quite different. Her gift to Aaron would cost her a $500,000 deduction from her lifetime credit, leaving her only $1,500,000 to cover the remaining $2,000,000 in her estate. Estate taxes on $500,000 of her estate would be due at a 37 percent tax rate.

Income Taxes

In addition to the taxes discussed above, there may also be the issue of income taxes to resolve. Income taxes become an important issue as they relate to the transfer of any tax-deferred retirement or other tax-deferred assets. Such assets include 401(k)s or Individual Retirement Accounts (IRAs). Income tax issues also apply when there is a transfer of appreciated property or property that has increased in value since its original pur-chase date, which will trigger a capital gains tax.

There is a monumental amount of confusion when it comes to tax issues surrounding estate planning. In addition to doing your own research, it would be wise to seek counsel from a pro-fessional who has a thorough knowledge of gift, estate, inherit-ance, capital gains, and income tax issues. Understand that there are many accountants who don't deal with gift and estate taxes.

Appreciated Property

The issue of appreciated property, or property that has increased in value, is another tax-related consideration in estate planning.

The main issue that must be dealt with when it comes to appreciated property has to do with the property's "basis" or "cost-basis." Cost-basis is the amount paid for the property, plus the cost of improvements, minus any depreciation (or tax write-offs) taken up to the date of transfer. A step up in cost-basis occurs when a property is inherited or received by right of survivorship through joint tenancy. If the property is inherited, it is deemed that the recipient's cost-basis is 100 percent of the market value at the time of the death of the original owner. Thus it gets "stepped up" from the owner's original basis, which would have been the amount paid for the property. This would not happen if the owner made a gift of this same property during his or her lifetime. In that case the cost-basis in the gifted property remains the same and does not receive a step up for the donee (the one who receives the gift).

Cost-basis is affected by the way property is transferred. Consider the following three scenarios:
1) If I give 100 percent of a certain property to you during my lifetime, with no strings attached, it is a gift. Your cost-basis for that property would be the same as mine was when I gave it to you. If you then sell the property, your capital gains tax would be identical to mine.
2) If I transfer 50 percent of the property to you as a joint tenant, you receive all of it when I die. Your cost-basis on the half

you "own" as a joint tenant remains the same as in the above gift. However, the half you receive when I die gets a stepped-up cost-basis to the fair market value of the property on the date of my death. If you then sell the property, you would be subject to a capital gains tax on 50 percent of the appreciated value of the property.

3) If I give the entire property to you as an inheritance after my death, you get a new cost-basis on the entire property, stepped-up to the fair market value on the date of my death. A sale of the property at that time would incur no capital gains tax. Capital gains tax is calculated on the amount of money received on the sale, less the cost-basis. If you sell the property soon after you inherit it, you will pay zero capital gains tax, since your cost-basis in the entire property has stepped-up to the fair market value (which is the same as the sales price).

The above examples apply to all appreciated property, including stocks, bonds, and real estate. If the property is a business or investment property, then the amount of any depreciation taken during the holding period must be deducted from the original cost-basis. Due to this, investment property held for a long period of time often has no cost-basis left in it. That being the case, the entire sales price will be taxable if the original owner sells the property. This tax problem can sometimes totally discourage the sale of some highly appreciated non-residential assets.

In the instance of a residence that is not depreciable, in most cases the cost-basis is the purchase price plus the cost of any improvements. So the appreciation the property has experienced during the holding period is nearly all taxable. However, as you may know, owners of residential property have certain large exemptions available to them upon sale. A gift transfer of the property destroys these exemptions and, thus, is usually not advisable. In most cases, in order for it to be tax effective and appropriate, the gifting of appreciated property requires professional planning.

For instance, Ralph bought stock in the late '50s and held it until we met him in the early '90s. This stock did not pay dividends. So the only benefit was its appreciated value, or increase in the price of the stock, which had risen astronomically over the years. Ralph didn't think he could afford to sell the stock because his taxes would be so high. However, he was leery of the alternative. He was a millionaire several times over on paper, but he was having a hard time making ends meet. He was living extremely modestly and needed additional income.

With special handling, situations like this can be solved and the tax avoided altogether. At the same time, this type of planning is complicated and may require a gift to a charity. Ralph had a few choices. He could sell the stock and pay the taxes, he could make a donation that would benefit both himself and a charity, or he could continue to scrimp and save and stay hard-pressed and miserable. Since he opted for the latter of the three, we presume that his heirs will enjoy the benefit of the wealth he has accumulated.

Inherited Property Gets a New Cost-Basis

When appreciated property is inherited, it gets a new cost-basis. Thus, inheriting property is by far the best way to acquire highly appreciated property because the heir can sell the property without being saddled with the capital gains tax that the predecessor would have had to pay. The problem with this scenario is that somebody has to die. Nevertheless, <u>for many estates, giving the heirs an inheritance is the best way to distribute appreciated property for tax reasons</u>.

Asset Protection

In addition to concerns regarding taxes, the idea of asset protection is playing a larger and larger part in estate planning. In fact, it has been suggested that an attorney's failure to advise his or her clients of asset protection issues is unethical and, perhaps, even actionable. If an activity is actionable, it simply means that it could subject the actor to being sued in a court of law for damages.

<u>In today's society,</u> especially in the United States, <u>it seems as if people are being sued for the most innocent conduct, with plaintiffs being awarded millions of dollars as a result</u>. In this "sue happy" environment, asset protection has become of great concern. In addition, asset-protection planning has an element of privacy many find refreshing in this day of open snooping into all areas of our personal lives.

Elements of asset protection are found in even the simplest forms of estate planning. For example, the revocable living trust, which we will discuss in greater detail later, is a simple estate planning option that offers protection against the unnecessary costs of probate. At first blush, it would seem that this trust is lacking other types of asset protection, but this is not necessarily true. The revocable living trust protects a surviving spouse's interest from tax by using a decedent's trust. Also the beneficiaries' interest is protected from creditors because the trust becomes irrevocable upon the death of the original trustors. In a later discussion of the revocable living trust, we will explore some of the beneficial asset protection possibilities.

Some people go even further to protect their assets from creditors and against lawsuits. Domestically, the Family Limited Partnership is traditionally used for such protection. Sometimes individuals gain additional asset protection by forming a corporation or an L.L.C. (Limited Liability Company). Those who want the "Cadillac" of all asset protection turn to offshore avenues, which range from offshore trusts to international business corporations to private annuities. Planning in the offshore arena is not for the fainthearted or the uninformed. Our advice is to use only the most experienced legal counsel in structuring this type of plan.

It's true that there are some good, solid offshore planning opportunities that will stand up to the most vigorous scrutiny by creditors, and that can, in fact, provide tax-planning benefits that are in compliance with IRS code. However, while some may be above board, many more of these offshore plans are unscrupulous and depend upon secrecy and illegal methods. Avoid these like the plague.

Good planning in the offshore area is expensive and should not be undertaken unless the estate is large enough to have substantial liquid assets that aren't needed for comfortable maintenance and support or for running the business domestically. Although it's perfectly acceptable and legal to use this type of planning for future asset protection and for tax benefits, offshore planning should never be used to defraud creditors or to evade income taxes. Such fraudulent activity is a sure recipe for disaster.

In the following chapters, we will be touching on various planning techniques, pointing out their tax-saving and asset-protection features. However, before you go on to the next chapters, we suggest that you make a list of the assets you now own and estimate what they are worth. On the next page we have included a list of assets you should consider and a way to evaluate them. Then, consider how long you have owned some of the assets and what you paid to acquire them. This will prepare you for the discussion that follows and will certainly prepare you for future discussions you may have with estate planning professionals.

CLIENT STATEMENT OF ASSETS

DESCRIPTION	MKT VALUE	AMOUNT OWED	NET VALUE
REAL PROPERTY	$_____	$_____	$_____
PERSONAL PROPERTY	$_____	$_____	$_____
CHECKING	$_____	$_____	$_____
SAVINGS/CDs	$_____	$_____	$_____
STOCKS/BONDS	$_____	$_____	$_____
IRA/PENSION FUNDS	$_____	$_____	$_____
LIFE INSURANCE	$_____	$_____	$_____
PERSONAL EFFECTS	$_____	$_____	$_____
FURNITURE	$_____	$_____	$_____
BUSINESS INTERESTS	$_____	$_____	$_____
PARTNERSHIPS	$_____	$_____	$_____
OTHER ASSETS	$_____	$_____	$_____
TOTAL ASSETS	$_____	$_____	$_____

I/we hereby state that the above is the estimated value of the assets in my estate and that A. Jeanne Emanuel may rely on this estimate in preparing a Revocable Living Trust to shelter my estate from Probate and Federal Inheritance Tax.

DATE_____ CLIENT SIGNATURE _____

CHAPTER 5

DOING NOTHING

Unfortunately, the most prevalent and popular estate plan used in the United States today is known as the "Do Nothing Plan." Using this plan is simple: All you have to do is sit back and do nothing. Then, when you die, the state you live in will apply its preset guidelines and take care of your estate by transferring your assets as it sees fit. <u>Doing nothing is a popular means of communicating. Yet, what do you think using the Do Nothing Plan says to your heirs?</u>

People get themselves into the Do Nothing Plan predicament for many reasons. They may think, "I won't be here, so what do I care?" or "I don't own enough property to require a plan." While the reasons may be valid in some cases, most often they are merely excuses that stem from fear or just plain ignorance.

Many people choose the Do Nothing Plan simply because they are confused about their options. Perhaps they assume that if they do nothing the state will distribute their estate satisfactorily through the probate process. They may figure there is no need for them to put in the time and expense of planning.

We know people who have large estates but who have no relatives or other individuals they care to name as heirs. A few people truly have no reason to plan their estate, but this is rare. While some people may not have blood relatives or close friends to whom they wish to bestow their possessions, <u>almost everyone has a charitable interest or deserving cause they want to support</u>. Most people don't want to die and leave their estate for the government to take everything.

Others, especially if they are younger than 50, don't think they will exit this world for a long time. They think they have plenty of time and don't feel the need to plan now. They may procrastinate because that is their nature or because they don't want to spend the money for such planning. Large houses and fancy cars seem to be more important. Some are waiting until the "perfect" time, or, as they put it, "until they get all their ducks in a row."

We hope their crystal ball is better than ours. From experience, we have learned that tragedy can strike without warning, and in many cases, the worst part of the tragedy is the mess some people leave behind because they have failed to plan for their own death. Often the people who seem the most foolhardy and casual in their approach are those who are the most in need of planning because they have spouses and dependent children. These people may buy life insurance, but often they won't finish the job of planning for the care and wealth of those who will receive the proceeds of the policy—the surviving spouse and the children.

While there seem to be some reasons that favor the Do Nothing Plan, we believe these reasons pale when weighed against the stress, trouble, and expense this lack of planning causes—not to mention the poor last impression left with the loved ones who are the victims of this plan. When it comes right down to it, the reasons for doing nothing really don't matter. What you must realize is that by <u>choosing the Do Nothing Plan, you are, in fact, making a choice and you are sending a communication to your heirs</u>. The message is loud and clear. To would-be heirs, a Do Nothing Plan most often says, "I don't care enough about your welfare to plan the distribution of my estate. You get the hassle of cleaning up all my mess for me." Doing nothing could also be interpreted as saying, "I didn't do anything, so now you can't blame me if things don't come out the way they should." The passing-the-buck game doesn't work well in this arena.

About the only time the Do Nothing Plan works well is when all of the assets are titled to the respective spouses in such a way that everything passes to the surviving spouse, as was the intent of both of them. However, a pattern has then been established, and the surviving spouse will probably die without a plan too. Then, everything will have to go to the surviving children or other heirs through the probate process defined by state laws.

The following real-life situations provide concrete examples of the damage that can be done with the Do Nothing Plan. Take the case in which the husband dies first, leaving everything to his wife, then add a small twist. Assume that, as is prevalent in today's society, the wife remarries and her new husband has children from a former marriage. The wife puts all of her assets together with her new husband's, and she suddenly dies without a plan. He gets everything. In all probability, to whom will he leave the estate? He'll leave it to his children, of course. Even if he doesn't give everything to his children and chooses to adopt the Do Nothing Plan his wife had, this sets up an unfavorable situation between the two sets of stepchildren. How would you feel if it had been your mother who remarried and left you with this Do Nothing Plan?

Here's another situation: Suppose a couple lives in a state that is not a community property state. One spouse dies with a Do Nothing Plan in place. Does the other spouse get all of the property automatically? Not necessarily. It depends on the laws of the state in which the two live. In some states, the spouse gets a lump sum allowance plus a percentage of the estate, and the remainder goes to the children of the departed. In such cases, the spouse may be named the representative of the estate, but the money that goes to any minor children will most likely be held for them by the state's probate court. The mother will likely be appointed as conservator for the children (but not always), and she will be subject to an expensive bond and burdensome requirements for reporting to the court exactly how she uses the money for the benefit of the children.

You want more fun? What if the above scenario applied to a second marriage, in which his children, her children, and their children are involved? What if the departed had been supporting an elderly parent? This dependent would receive none of the inheritance since under the state's law, he or she would not be an heir.

What happens if there's an accident, and both Mom and Dad die at the same time, leaving minor children and a Do Nothing Plan? Let's give the children a break and assume the estate is fairly large due to insurance proceeds. So at least money is not a problem. However, the court is going to decide who will take physical care of the children. The court is going to appoint a legal guardian. This person could be someone whom the parents would not have appointed, even under the worst of circumstances, to take care of their children. The court's decision won't be based on personal longtime knowledge, but on which candidate makes the best impression on the judge through written evidence and a brief observation at a hearing.

In such a case, the court will also appoint a conservator of the estate to manage the money and will require bonding and reporting until the children reach the age of majority. This conservator may be the same person as the guardian or may be a different person altogether. The cost of all this court supervision, not to mention the original probate fees, depletes the children's estate. When the children reach the age of majority, all of the money will have to be turned over to the children to do with as they please. In most cases, this is age eighteen. Would you want your children, at age eighteen, to have large amounts of money to spend however they want?

It seems obvious. The Do Nothing Plan is not the way to get the best results. The state's guidelines simply weren't fashioned with your personal needs or the best interests of your heirs in mind. So rather than falling into the Do Nothing Plan and leaving your estate planning up to the state, it would be wise to explore your options and discuss your goals with a professional estate planning attorney.

We have provided some examples showing how the Do Nothing Plan doesn't work in the legal sense. However, sometimes the plan works legally, but there are other major problems. For example, Bill is a 70-year-old widower. When his wife died, everything was transferred to him without probate. Bill has four children, and he wants the estate to go to them in equal shares when he dies. He has been told that the state's plan will do this for him. He chooses the Do Nothing Plan since it's cheap and easy.

Bill makes no other arrangements for his death. He never mentions these matters to any of his children, and they don't bring up the idea of estate planning either. He loves them all equally and feels they already know this. He only has moderate assets. He owns his home, and he has some credit card bills, a couple of bank accounts, a life insurance policy, and some savings bonds. The estate is valued at $400,000. All bank accounts are in his name alone. He dies.

There is no money available to pay for the funeral and the burial. It is all tied up in Bill's accounts, and nobody can get to it. Bill's oldest son, Fred, has to cover most of the expense since the others can't afford it. Some of the children want an expensive and elaborate funeral. Others want the simplest service possible. They compromise and plan a moderate affair. Nobody is really satisfied, and it is still very expensive. A probate procedure is required in order to obtain title to the assets in Bill's estate. Bill had an automobile, some fairly expensive jewelry, family heirlooms, china and silver, and the normal furniture and clothing items. Bill's children can't agree on how the personal items should be distributed, and some of them think things are missing from the list, including a valuable coin collection, two nice paintings, and a bank account.

Fred hires the attorney who has begun the probate process to help straighten things out, and Fred is appointed as the personal representative for the estate. He will be entitled to receive a statutory fee for his services, and so will the attorney. The combined fees will be approximately 6-10 percent of the total value of the gross estate. One of the brothers, Sam, is not happy about Fred being named as the representative. Sam feels he was closer to his father and thinks he should be in charge. The two sisters think Sam absconded with the coin collection and the paintings. They also think Sam coerced Bill into transferring money into Sam's account before he died.

Fred does his best to make a fair distribution of most of the personal items, such as jewelry, clothing, and furnishings, but his siblings are unhappy with their shares. Fred finally sells the car because the heirs can't reach an agreement about how much the car is worth or if one of them should receive it. His sisters and brother think Fred sold it too cheaply, and they are angry because the whole probate process is taking so long and is becoming so expensive. Together, the other children hire an attorney and file a suit to have Fred removed as the representative of the estate and to have an audit of the estate's assets.

After two long years, the lawsuit and the estate are finally set-tled. Once all the expenses are deducted, there is less than $250,000 remaining to be shared among the heirs. Funeral and burial expenses, attorney fees, fees for the personal representa-tive, court costs, appraisal fees, taxes, real estate closing costs, and other expenses eat up more than $35,000 of each child's inheritance. Even more tragic, the siblings no longer trust or respect each other as much as they did before this process began. In fact, the family is so split that the rift between Fred and his siblings may never heal.

What was the result of the Do Nothing Plan in this case? Did it provide what the departed wanted? Yes, in a way, it did. As Bill wanted, the estate was divided equally among his children. Yet here is the question: Was that all Bill wanted? We doubt it. We believe he would have wanted his kids to think that he was a great guy, that he loved and cherished them equally, and that he had done his best for them.

Did the plan he chose do that? Not in our professional opinion. By doing nothing, this father's last communication with his children caused them pain, anger, resentment, and bitterness. His plan worked legally, at least after a fashion. However, it ended up costing his heirs financially and emotionally. What kind of impression was this to leave with his children?

Here's another example: Jeanne and Karen, her friend, were talking about estate planning one day, and Karen indicated that her father had died a few years ago. Her father and grandfather had both been very wealthy. However, her father had not managed his affairs well during his life. When he died, he had no plan in place. Taxes and creditors took the entire estate, leaving Karen and her mother destitute.

This had happened 15 years ago, and when Jeanne asked Karen how the experience made her feel about her father, she blinked her eyes and replied, "I am real ticked off at him. Why didn't he love us enough to take care of these things? My mother and I depended on him. We weren't even prepared to take care of ourselves because he had always told us we had nothing to worry about in the money department. I think he played a really dirty trick on me, and I don't know why he did it."

We wish we had a nickel for each of the people we have talked to who have said, "Oh, if only my mother (or father) had cared enough to have a plan in place that would have helped us through their departure. I just can't tell you the trouble it would have saved."

Now, look at the list of assets you made in the previous chapter. Do you have so few assets that you need no plan at all? What message will you leave your loved ones when you die if you don't make an effort to have a loving last communication in place?

Now, here's the good news. There are many alternatives to the Do Nothing Plan. While some are only slightly better, some of them are really great. The point is there are numerous ways to

Do Something—any of which are better than taking no type of estate planning action at all.

CHAPTER 6

A LETTER TO THE JUDGE

Many people realize that the Do Nothing Plan isn't a wise choice. The next most popular method to transfer an estate is writing a letter to the judge of the probate court. The letter is called a last will and testament, or simply referred to as a will. For hundreds of years, most people who have done anything at all about planning their estate_even those people who are the most knowledgeable and the wealthiest_have resorted to using a last will and testament as their sole means of estate planning.

Celebrities and well-known people, such as billionaire Howard Hughes and U.S. Supreme Court Justice Warren Burger, have relied on these legal letters of transfer for their estate planning. In the case of Howard Hughes, more than thirty different versions of documents purporting to be his will were submitted to the probate courts in California, Nevada, and Texas. After many lengthy trials, none of these documents were ever admitted to probate, and what was left after taxes and attorney's fees passed intestate to his distant relatives, whom Howard barely knew. Burger's estate incurred many thousands of dollars in unnecessary taxes and other costs because he relied on a handwritten (holographic) will for his estate plan. Though many other notable people have used this way of planning, it's obvious from these examples that a will may not accomplish the intended results or be the most satisfactory communication with one's heirs.

So, what is a last will and testament, and how does it work? The last will and testament is a letter to the probate judge asking for approval of the way an individual wishes to distribute property to his or her heirs and beneficiaries. The judge responds to the letter by opening a procedure called "probate." Probate is a court process with all of the legal antics that are attached to such proceedings. The first thing that happens in probate is the executor of the will, now known as the "representative of the estate," must go to the trouble and expense of hiring an attorney. This attorney must present the representative of the estate to the court for approval to serve in that capacity before the representative can proceed.

Understand that the will does not start out with the salutation, "Dear Judge." A will is a very formal document that must conform to the rules and regulations set out by the legislature of the state where an individual lives at the time of death. On top of the state's regulations, there are numerous court rules that apply in the county court that administers the estate. If a will does not comply with all of the rules, the judge will declare the will invalid, and the proceedings will go on as though such a document had not been drafted in the first place.

In most states, various forms of wills are recognized as legal. For example, most states acknowledge a written, formal will that is properly prepared by an attorney and witnessed by the prescribed number of witnesses. In addition, states will uphold holographic wills, wills prepared by the person making the will without an attorney. However, if a state is to recognize a holographic will, the letter must follow strict rules established by the probate code. Therefore using a holographic will is a risky procedure and should be avoided whenever possible. <u>Many people think preparing a will is simple and easy, but this perception is false</u>. While wills do contain some standard language, they must be individualized for each situation, person, state, and county. Consequently, wills (especially those created using fill-in-the-blank style templates) should be reviewed by an estate planning attorney to avoid unintended results.

Another word of caution: A will should not be made at the insistence of another person, even if the prodding person is one's child or a good friend. We have seen cases in which not just one, but several different "form" wills were signed by a testator at the insistence of caretakers or children. Each purported to be valid, each claimed to be the last executed document, and each called for distribution that was inconsistent and incompatible with the other documents. Situations such as these lead to expensive will contests that create bitterness and strife among the heirs. Usually, only the attorneys win in these cases. Such do-it-yourself wills are treated with skepticism by the courts because these kinds of documents have traditionally been a breeding ground for trickery and scams.

In addition to formal and holographic wills, oral wills (also known as deathbed wills) are recognized in some states, but only in the direst of emergency circumstances. Their accepted use is so limited that we are not going to give further discussion to this method of estate planning.

Wills, whether formal or holographic, may be written as simple wills, joint wills, mirror wills, or as complicated wills with multiple tax provisions or combined with trusts that are to be created upon the death of the will's maker. <u>Regardless of the structure and nature, all wills share one thing in common: They all have to be probated</u>. In other words, every will goes to the judge of the probate court who controls the estate from the beginning of the procedure until the end, which can sometimes take years.

What Is Probate? Why Is It Needed?

Probate is a legal procedure designed to pass title of a departed individual's property on to the legal heirs. Heirs are those persons who, by virtue of their bloodline, are entitled to have the property, or they are those persons designated in a will as the persons to receive the property. <u>In its simplest form, probate is all about passing title to property.</u>

The probate court is usually a separate division of the state's Superior Court. It is staffed by the probate judge(s) and probate examiners, who are attorneys who assist the judge. Probate court approves wills, appoints the representatives of the estate, and supervises the administration of the estate. This means that the court oversees the duties of notifying creditors, paying debts, liquidating property, operating businesses, paying taxes, resolving disputes, handling challenges to the will, and facilitating final distribution of the assets. The probate court has jurisdiction over trust disputes and is also in charge of appointing and supervising conservators and guardians of the estates of persons who are incompetent because of age or health disabilities. Even though there have been attempts in most states to streamline the probate process, it is still a lengthy, expensive, stressful experience for heirs to go through. Probate court is a busy place, and it is the only way that property legally belonging to a person who has died can be transferred to the proper heirs, since the person on the title is deceased and no longer able to sign the title over. Basically, that's what the whole process of probate boils down to—a signature!

Even with the hassles of probate, we feel that leaving a will is a much better option than the Do Nothing Plan. So we'll explain here a little about how this type of estate planning works.

As noted above, there can be drawbacks when taking the do-it-yourself route in drafting a will. Since self-service wills can have situational or state-specific flaws, we believe the first thing a person needs to do when preparing a will is to see an attorney who specializes in estate planning. It used to be that any attorney could prepare a simple will, but the world has changed. Today, unless they specifically practice in this very complicated area of the law, most attorneys no longer undertake this task. Even the simplest will requires specialized knowledge. In fact, the need for specialized knowledge is true for all types of estate planning and in all other areas of law today.

Unfortunately, we have seen cases where people have been poorly advised about estate planning by professionals in other fields, even by respected attorneys who practice very well in other areas of the law. We suggest you get the right advice from the right professional before making decisions about your plan. For instance, Jeanne, who is a very experienced estate planning attorney, would not be the right attorney to assist you with a divorce.

This concept makes sense. You would not go to a plumber to treat an earache; you'd go to a doctor. You may even go to an ear specialist for the best care. If you went to your accountant or your insurance agent or your financial planner to do your primary estate planning, you wouldn't receive the most appropriate advice. Notice we say primary planning here. People who are knowledgeable in these other fields should, indeed, be included as part of a complete planning team. However, it should be an estate planning attorney who advises you about the legal documents you need and then prepares those documents for you, or reviews them if you have created them yourself or with the help of a fill-in-the-blank type template. There are a few excellent software programs to assist you with making estate planning decisions. Use of any of these in preparation for the first consultation with an estate planning attorney is extremely valuable as a preliminary planning tool.

In cases where there are no children and very little property, a simple will could possibly suffice. Estate planning in such cases is basically a matter of designating who will receive the assets and who will be the representative. However, where there is a substantial amount of property and complicated tax issues, a more comprehensive plan will be necessary in order to comply with the tax laws and save money for the estate. This is especially true when there is an ongoing business or when other complicated business affairs are involved. When there are dependents to be considered, a last will and testament is advisable, but additional estate planning is necessary to fully plan for your heirs' future.

While using a will as your sole means of estate planning is certainly better than doing nothing, it isn't extremely beneficial in most cases. There is no privacy in using a will. <u>Once it is filed, a will becomes a matter of public record, open to anyone's scrutiny</u>. It is simple to challenge a will, which can subject all parties concerned to lengthy and expensive litigation. The court takes total control of the estate during the administration period, which often lasts for years. This may even mean that your heirs will have to petition the court for an allowance to cover living expenses during this time. True, a will may be a little better than doing nothing, but other methods of estate planning are far superior, produce better results, and are less expensive in the long run.

CHAPTER 7

OTHER ALTERNATIVES

It's pretty simple to discount the Do Nothing Plan, and it's equally as easy to see that the infamous will may not be all it's touted to be. Because this is true, many people use other methods as an alternative or in addition to the will. Most of these are effective for only limited purposes or sometimes even have detrimental unintended consequences.

These alternative plans include gifting, charitable giving, joint tenancy, pre-designated beneficiaries, and retirement plans. Let's explore each of these limited options to discover both their positive and negative aspects.

GIFTING

"Why don't we just give the house (or some money) to the kids now, while we're still around?" This question represents a common but somewhat misguided notion that we hear more frequently than we would like. However, don't get us wrong. Having someone ask us that question is a lot better than hearing that it has already been done!

You may be wondering, what exactly is wrong with the idea of giving your assets to your children while you're still alive? This might seem like a good way to avoid probate, but it's important to understand the tax laws before taking this step. When planning to gift property, the tax effect on both the giver and receiver of the property should be taken into account. Further, the giver must also contemplate the loss of control of the property_and even possible loss of the property_because of the liabilities and outstanding debt of the receiver. Liability issues will be explored in greater detail later in this chapter when we discuss joint tenancy planning.

Tax considerations vary depending upon what type of property is being gifted. If the gift is cash or its equivalent, the giver may need to consider whether any "gift tax" may be incurred. If the gift is property (such as real estate or stocks or bonds that have been held by the giver for a period of time and are highly appreciated in value), an analysis should be done to determine how such a gift affects the receiver's cost-basis. (See the prior discussion on cost-basis and appreciated property.) In addition to tax issues, other issues may be a factor. It is important to understand that if the giver plans to maintain possession and control of the property, the issue of whether it was really a gift may arise and the property could be brought back into the estate for estate tax purposes.

These issues must be analyzed in light of the reason for making the gift. If the gift is being given strictly for the purpose of avoiding probate or avoiding estate tax, alternative methods should be explored. One possible tax consequence must be weighed against the other. In thinking this through, the receiver's relationship to the giver is also a factor. If the receiver is a spouse, all of the consequences will be different than if the receiver is a child, friend, or charitable institution.

As you can see, this is a rather complicated area that deserves the professional attention of someone well-versed in each of the specific problems that may arise in each individual instance.

Sometimes people give a gift and don't even realize it. Several years ago, Edward and Anna visited Jeanne about transferring a parcel of real estate to one of their children. For various reasons, the two had agreed that their son, Walter, would pay them about half of the market value for this property. They believed this arrangement would be ideal. It would reduce the capital gains tax Edward and Anna would have to pay, and it would benefit their son. In addition, Walter could take the fair market value of the property for his cost-basis if, and when, he sold it.

They didn't realize they could be setting themselves, or Walter, up for some major tax problems if this transaction were to be audited by the IRS. They didn't think about the fact that the one-half value they weren't going to require Walter to pay would be considered a gift to him. Nor did they realize that the IRS could come back at a later date and challenge the value of the property at the time the gift was made. The transaction, in fact, would be a part-gift/part-sale transaction and would need to be based on the appraised value of the property at the time of the transfer to Walter.

Taking Jeanne's advice, Edward and Anna had the property appraised. Then, they entered into a simple sales agreement with Walter. The agreement outlined the entire transaction, designating the portion of the sale and the portion of the gift and accounting for the full value of the property. Of the transfer price, $40,000 was then credited against their annual exclusion (which was $10,000 at that time) from gift tax—$10,000 each from Edward and Anna to Walter and $10,000 each to Walter's wife, Susan. The balance of the gift portion was credited against their combined lifetime exclusion of $1,350,000 (which was $675,000 each at that time). This left the parents an ample exclusion amount to offset any projected estate taxes upon their death.

Using a portion of their combined exemption of $1,350,000 was appropriate and beneficial in this instance, and no tax was due on this transaction. An appropriate gift tax return was filed, documenting this entire transaction. A simple and inexpensive solution accomplished what the parties desired without the fear of future complications.

CHARITABLE GIFTING

Another form of giving used in estate planning is called charitable gifting. Not only is this a good way to avoid capital gains and inheritance taxes, but we are of the opinion that gifting property or money to a charity is a commendable thing to do. As part of a simple plan, it's very easy to leave a small portion of an estate to a favorite charity. All that is required is to make a provision in the will or trust naming the charity as the beneficiary of a stated sum of money or of a small percentage of the total estate. It may surprise you to know that in most of the cases we have seen, the heirs have supported this type of gift.

In some instances, charitable gifting is used to avoid capital gains tax on highly appreciated property when the grantors wish to sell that property and generate income for themselves during their lifetimes. In this case the property is transferred to a charitable remainder trust, naming a qualified charity as the beneficiary of the trust upon the grantor's death. After this transfer is made, the trustee sells the property and invests the proceeds to produce income to the grantors, in accordance with the provisions of the trust document. The grantors do not pay any capital gains tax on the sale, and they get an income tax deduction based on the value of the property donated to the charity. In addition, the former non-income-producing property that was transferred to the charity now generates income for the grantor. This is a sweet deal in many respects for the grantors because they can be the trustees of the trust, and in some cases, they may be able to retain the power to change the charity they have chosen and designate another charity to receive the property.

There is only one fly in the ointment. What about the grantors' heirs? How do they like this deal? Not very much! Upon the death of the grantors, the assets the heirs would have received will now go to a charity. Most heirs would be very unhappy with this result. The good news is that there is a solution to this problem. That is to take a portion of the income generated by the charitable remainder trust and buy life insurance on the grantors. When the grantors die, the children receive from the insurance company the amount they would have received had they inherited the property directly. This kind of plan works well when there is a large estate that would incur capital gains tax on the original sale of the property by the grantors, as well as inheritance tax on the property upon the grantors' death. Obviously, this is not a do-it-yourself plan, but one that requires consultation with and assistance from professionals who understand the intricacies of charitable gifting.

Another note as you contemplate adding the gifting component to your estate plan is to <u>remember that a gift is a gift is a gift</u>. What we mean by this is that making a true gift is permanent and cannot be undone. Therefore, when you give assets as a gift, you give up total control over these assets forever. They no longer belong to you. So, in that sense, this type of planning is the best asset protection you can get. You no longer own the assets, and providing you haven't broken any laws and fraudulently transferred the assets, your creditors can not get to them. As illustrated by the above discussion, giving to an individual or charity may have more than the intrinsic rewards of such an act. Indeed, charitable giving offers estate planning benefits as well. In fact, even the government applauds charitable gifting, and Uncle Sam smiles on such grantors with a gift in return: a tax break.

JOINT TENANCY PLANNING

Joint tenancy planning is very common. In fact, there are two types of joint ownership that are often confused. One is joint tenancy, which always includes the right of survivorship, and the other is tenants in common, which does not. This simply means that with the right to survivorship, the asset is passed as a matter of law to the other joint owners upon the death of one of the joint tenants. On the other hand, tenants in common may will their share of the property to their heirs or, if they die intestate, it will automatically go to their estate. This means that probate is avoided by holding property as joint tenants with the right of survivorship. That is about the only benefit of this strategy as an estate planning tool.

People are told that if they put their property in joint tenancy it will avoid probate. This is very true, but that's only the good news. The bad news is that by choosing to place someone else on the asset title in this fashion, the original owner gives up control of that asset and negates the tax benefits available with other types of planning. By choosing joint tenancy, original owners are no longer free to leave even what would seem to be their half of the property to whomever they wish, and they have subjected the entire amount of the property to another person's liabilities, whatever those liabilities may be.

We'll illustrate with Maggie's story. Maggie is a widow in her late 70s who now needs a little assistance in handling her own affairs. Maggie has three children: two daughters and a son. She owns her own home, which is located in a fast-growing beach community, so its value has skyrocketed. (It's now valued at about $1,200,000.) In addition, Maggie has a couple of bank accounts (one checking and one savings account) and two CDs. These accounts are valued at a total of $250,000.

When Maggie's husband died about two years ago, friends told Maggie that she should put her children on the deed so her estate wouldn't have to go to probate. Maggie also added her daughter, Jennifer, to her bank accounts. Maggie did this so

Jennifer could assist her with her affairs if she got sick. Maggie wants Jennifer to pay any last expenses and then share the balance of the money in the accounts equally with the other children. Maggie has no other estate plan. What's going to happen when Maggie dies?

There are a couple of possible scenarios.
Scenario No.1
Maggie dies, and the house is sold. The three children split the proceeds from the sale of the house equally. Jennifer pays Maggie's last expenses and then splits the remaining $210,000 in the bank accounts with her brother and sister. All goes well, except that Jennifer may have a problem. Legally, she inherited the money from her mother's bank accounts. Then she made gifts of $70,000 to each of her two siblings. Jennifer's accountant explains that this may cause a tax problem. Jennifer is not a happy camper, and Maggie certainly had no intention for this to happen when she made her plans.

Scenario No. 2
What if, under this scenario, Jennifer simply refuses to distribute the remaining amounts in her mother's accounts? The money is legally hers, and since there was no plan in place to dispute that result, Jennifer's brother and sister would most likely be out of luck. It's sad, but true. We have seen this type of thing happen! What kind of rapport would this leave between the children? What's Maggie's final communication to her children?

Scenario No. 3

During Maggie's lifetime, Jennifer has an auto accident in which the driver of the other car is severely injured. Jennifer has minimum insurance coverage, and there is a judgment rendered against her in excess of the policy limits. The judgment creditor executes against the bank accounts and effectively takes them all, since, as a joint tenant, Jennifer has the right to the money at any time. In addition, the judgment creditor liens the house and forces the property to be sold to satisfy the judgment. The home sells as a distress sale, and the property brings $850,000, of which the creditor takes 25 percent. What's the result? Now Maggie is homeless, and she has only her share of the proceeds of the house left in her name. What does she do now?

Scenario No. 4

Jennifer gets married to a man who turns out to be a guitar-playing beach bum. The marriage doesn't work out. As part of the divorce settlement, the bum claims the joint tenancy property is community property and that half of Jennifer's share belongs to him. The court agrees. Now Maggie has him as a partner, as well.

Are these scenarios far-fetched? No, each is well within the realm of the possible. Actually, they represent only a few of the pitfalls and the frightful end results that could occur from using joint tenancy as an estate planning tool. Unfortunately, joint tenancy has been routinely used in banking and real estate circles for many years. Advising clients to use this method comes almost automatically to bankers and realtors without much heed to potential drawbacks.

While there are some cases where title in joint tenancy may be desirable and appropriate, this can only be determined by someone who has a good understanding of the law and who conducts a thorough exploration of other alternatives. <u>The results of blindly choosing joint tenancy can be disastrous.</u>

Understand that joint tenancy has very few asset protection benefits because a creditor can still go after part or, in some cases, all of the assets. While seemingly simple and effective, joint tenancy can be another pitfall. All possible consequences should be thoroughly investigated before opting for this route.

PREDESIGNATED BENEFICIARIES

Certain types of assets are transferred by beneficiary designation, meaning the estate doesn't have to go through probate but automatically goes to the person or persons named to receive it. Remember, probate is all about title passing from the departed person to the heirs. Beneficiary designations are most commonly used with regard to life insurance, annuities and other types of insurance products. In some states, banking institutions and even brokerage houses are beginning to use the beneficiary designation.

Our experience with the latter is that even when the stock brokerage uses a beneficiary designation, stocks are still difficult to transfer to the heirs. It can be done, but it takes a lot of time, patience, and persistence. Again, in some instances, this may be a suitable planning option, but we feel it should be used with extreme care since the benefits are limited.

We want to take a moment to caution you. Recently, some brokerage firms and other institutions have begun introducing a Transfer on Death (TOD) Agreement. Be wary of this agreement and the benefits and consequences it may have on your estate. Do not be fooled by claims that this agreement guarantees your estate will avoid probate. Also ignore any guidelines that state you must have your assets held at these institutions.

RETIREMENT PLANS

Retirement plans, including IRAs, 401(k)s, and qualified pensions, are all passed to heirs under a beneficiary designation. These assets have definite tax benefits that are personal to the owner. However, once assets are transferred to another owner, those benefits are lost and negative tax consequences kick in. For that reason, these types of assets are always transferred by beneficiary designation upon the death of the owner and their ownership is never transferred to another entity.

All of these tax-deferred plans have some asset protection features. IRAs generally provide some protection from creditors (this varies from state to state) while IRS-qualified plans, such as 401(k)s provide total protection from creditors in almost every state. Although in many states these plans do include some asset-protection features, IRAs are not qualified plans, and they are generally not as complete with regard to creditors' rights as a qualified plan is. For this reason, it is advisable that employees attempt, if possible, to remain in their qualified plans even after retirement to take advantage of this protection. At this writing, the IRS is considering a change in the law mandating a change in the requirements for distribution at age 70 1/2, which could affect your plan. Check with your planner regarding this issue.

A QUICK CHECK

Now, take another look at the list of assets you have made. Do any of them include another person on the title besides you? Are there any items on your list that you might want to give away now? Remember, when you give something away, it cannot be taken back. Make a list of persons to whom you want to give your worldly goods.

Are there any charitable organizations you want to remember? What about your church, your lodge, or some other organization in your community? Do you have assets with large capital gains that are not providing you with income or that you can't sell because you would get hammered by the capital gains taxes? If so, then perhaps a charitable remainder trust is a possibility for you. Such trusts offer great benefits, both for you and for others. So if the situation fits, we recommend that you at least consider a charitable remainder trust and discuss this option with a knowledgeable estate planning attorney.

CHAPTER 8

TRUSTS IN GENERAL

The subject of trusts is extensive. While all trusts have certain basic characteristics, there are many different types of trusts. All trusts are created by a formal written agreement between the creators of the trust and the trustee (manager) of the trust. The trust agreement outlines all pertinent terms of the trust, including information about the parties, instructions to the trustee about how the trust is to be operated, and details about how the final distribution is to be made upon the settlement of the trust. The most common categories of trusts are revocable living trusts, life insurance trusts, and charitable remainder trusts.

Trusts may be either inter-vivos (created during the lifetime of the trustor) or testamentary (created at the death of the trustor). Trusts are said to be "funded" if the trust holds tangible assets or "unfunded" if the trust holds intangibles, such as life insurance policies. Every trust involves three parties: a trustor, a trustee, and a beneficiary. Every trust is either revocable or irrevocable. Trusts can be either domestic or foreign. Every trust is designed to fit a certain set of circumstances and to accomplish predefined purposes, and they often go by the name of their intended purpose. (These include the marital deduction trust, the bypass trust, the capital gains bypass trust, the irrevocable life insurance trust, the asset protection trust, the charitable remainder trust, and so on.) These trusts are all variations of the basic trust; their names merely describe their purpose.

In this chapter, we will discuss the basic characteristics of trusts. We will offer a broad discussion of a few specific types of trusts, such as irrevocable life insurance trusts and charitable remainder trusts. The revocable living trust won't be included in this chapter's discussion. Due to the importance of the revocable living trust as a primary estate planning tool, and the fact that we highly recommend it for most estate plans, several later chapters are devoted to presenting the details about this type of trust.

THE THREE TRUST POSITIONS
The Trustor

In any type of trust, the person who creates the trust is called the "grantor," the "trustor," or the "settlor." (We will use the title "trustor.") A trust can have more than one trustor, and often a husband and wife will be the co-trustors. The trustor creates the trust by stating the trust's purpose, what property is to be placed in it, who will be appointed as trustee(s), who the beneficiaries are to be, and how and when the beneficiaries will be entitled to receive the distribution of the assets. The trustor determines whether the trust will be revocable or irrevocable, as well as all other specific terms and conditions of the trust. The trustor instructs the trustee (manager) on how trust assets are to be managed during the existence of the trust and who is to receive the assets upon the termination of the trust.

In this last respect, the trust works like a last will and testament and has the same distribution clauses that might be found in a will. The difference is that the language will be broader and more flexible. One should think of the trustor(s) as the owner(s) of the trust. In many cases, trustors will reserve to themselves certain powers over the trust and its assets that no one else will have. These powers often include the right to amend the trust, change the beneficiaries, appoint the trustees and, if the trust is revocable, revoke it.

The Trustee

The trustee is the person or entity named by the trustor (owner) to manage the trust. A trust can have more than one trustee. In cases of multiple trustees, the trustees either act as co-trustees with regard to management of the entire trust or they act singularly as managers of separate activities of the same trust. In some cases, the trustor can also serve as the trustee. Think of the trustee of the trust as the person who is hired to manage the assets under the written direction of the trustor (owner).

A trustee must be over the age of 18 and should be well-qualified to administer all of the financial aspects of the trust. In choosing the trustee, careful consideration must be given to all aspects of the situation, since such a position imposes strenuous legal, moral, and fiscal responsibilities. If the trust is to be ongoing over a long period of time or if it is going to require the investment of large sums of money or the management of an ongoing business, close attention should particularly be given to the choice of the trustee. When an estate has complicated issues or requires ongoing responsibilities for a trustee, the services of an institutional trustee may need to be considered.

Sometimes it is prudent to appoint a corporate trustee, such as a bank or trust company. Many of the stock brokerage houses are now installing trust departments, which serve in this capacity so that investment continuity can be maintained. Sometimes such trustees will serve free of charge if the duties of the trustee are minimal, such as acting as the trustee of an unfunded life insurance trust until such time as the trust is actually funded with the proceeds of the policy.

Corporate trustees have specific guidelines under which they will serve, and if a corporate trustee is named, the trust will need to be tailored to meet such specifications. This is especially true of investment brokerages. There are other professional or private fiduciary trustees who can be appointed to serve and who are more flexible in their requirements. In one instance, when a trustee was required to wind up the affairs as the general partner of a family-limited partnership, a private professional fiduciary was willing to serve while most corporate trustees were not. It is not uncommon to have an individual trustee and a corporate trustee serve as co-trustees. A further discussion regarding trustee appointments will be undertaken in Chapter Eleven.

In most states trustees are entitled by law to receive reasonable fees for their services even if the trust instrument does not specifically provide for them. These fees are commonly calculated based on the same charges that a bank would charge—approximately 1 to 2 percent of the amount of the gross estate figured on an annual basis. The responsibility and liability alone often justify the fee, and in most cases, a trustee does more than enough work to earn the fees. While we do not encourage it, a trustee can always waive the right to receive a fee. This sometimes happens when a family member acts as trustee for a family trust.

The Beneficiary

Every trust has a beneficiary, which can be any person, place, or entity (even the family pet) or a combination of more than one of these choices. The beneficiaries are the receivers of the benefits of the trust. In other words, beneficiaries get to use or possess the assets of the trusts or they receive the trust property outright as a gift. There are many options for structuring the way the beneficiaries will benefit from the trust.

A beneficiary can be entitled, by virtue of the trust agreement, to enjoy only the use and possession of an asset, such as a home, a vacation house, a boat, or an airplane, for a specified period of time or for his or her lifetime. Sometimes the trust pays for the maintenance and support of such assets, and other times the beneficiary must maintain and support the asset during the period of time he or she has the use of it.

A beneficiary may receive only the right to reap the income generated by the principal of the trust. Sometimes, such a beneficiary may have the right to some of the principal of the trust as well, either at the discretion of the trustee or upon the occurrence of an event, such as an illness or other catastrophe. In these cases, there will be other beneficiaries named to receive the remainder of the assets when the first-named users are no longer entitled to them. These beneficiaries are known as remainder-men.

The trustor can make distribution of specific items of property to certain identified beneficiaries or can leave percentage interests in the trust property to individuals, groups of individuals, or other types of beneficiaries. (One example would call for leaving 25 percent of an estate to each of a trustor's four children.)

The trustor can direct that other trusts be created within the trust. There is no limit to the number of trusts that can be created in this fashion. A trust within a trust is often set up to take care of minor children or other dependents. Sometimes these types of trusts provide for outright distributions when the children reach a certain age. Other times, percentages are distributed as a child reaches certain age levels. For example, a child might receive 25 percent of the trust at age 25 and 50 percent of the remaining balance at age 30, with the full remaining balance at age 40. <u>Distribution schemes are limited only by the imagination of the trustor</u> and the feasibility of the ongoing management of the trust. However, the financial wisdom of keeping a trust going for long periods of time should always be considered. Are there going to be sufficient funds in the trust to warrant paying the trustee and filing tax returns? Will the assets of the trust generate enough money to justify the waiting period?

The beneficiary can be the trustor or even the trustee. As is often the case with a revocable living trust, the same person will hold all three positions (trustor, trustee and beneficiary) at the same time. In deciding who should hold these positions, it is wise to consult with a professional to determine the feasibility of the various options in light of the purpose of the trust. For example, there would be little value in forming an irrevocable trust in which the trustor, trustee, and beneficiary were all the same person if the purpose of the trust was to protect its assets from the trustor's creditors or to keep it out of the trustor's estate for tax purposes. The test of asset protection is always the control by the trustor: if the trustor can get to the asset, then so can the creditor.

Some beneficiaries may be disabled and unable to provide for themselves. In these cases, special-needs provisions can be added to the trust so that the person's existing public support or assistance benefits are not disturbed. Special-needs provisions must be carefully drafted in light of the current law in order to accomplish their very specialized purposes.

OTHER CHARACTERISTIC OF TRUSTS
Revocable Versus Irrevocable

Trusts are either revocable or irrevocable. If a trust is revocable, the trustor retains the right to alter or remove items from the trust at any time during his or her lifetime. When a trust is revocable it means that the trustor retains control over the trust assets. A trust is revoked when the trustor formally revokes it by a written declaration and removes the assets from the trust. This can be done partially—as in the case of a dissolution of a marriage, when one partner revokes the trust as to his or her interest in favor of the remaining partner—or in whole, when the total trust is revoked by all trustors.

One of the benefits of the revocable nature of this type of trust is the ability to take assets in and out of the trust at will without any significant tax consequences or other detriment to the trustor(s). In addition, almost anything about the trust may be changed during the lifetime of the trustor. This means the trustor can change the beneficiaries, the gifts to the beneficiaries, the appointed successor trustees, the current trustees, and anything else that suits the purpose of the trustor. These changes are accomplished by amending the original trust.

The other side of the coin is that in a revocable trust there is little, if any, asset protection afforded to the trustor of such trusts, and most tax benefits are lost as well. If the trust is irrevocable, the opposite is true to the extent that the trustor gives up control. For maximum asset protection and tax benefits, the trustor must retain virtually no incidents of ownership. This means that to protect assets, the trustor should not, in most cases, be the beneficiary, reserve the right to use assets transferred to the trust, receive income from the trust, or act as the trustee. If a trustor retains even minor ownership rights, such as the right to change the beneficiaries or the trustee of the trust, this can be enough to give rights to the trustors' creditors or to the IRS.

This is, by no means, an exhaustive list of these rights, and the drafter of any trust should research this area carefully in order to protect the trustors' purposes in creating the trust in the first place. Careful research is especially necessary if the trustors' purpose is to create asset protection from creditors and claimants, as well as to install tax shelter features.

One downside of the irrevocable trust is that, to be effective, it must be truly unchangeable. There can be no strings attached to the assets transferred to the trust. This means the trustor must not only give up control but also must relinquish all right, title, and interest in those assets forever. Many people balk at this requirement. It is certainly something that must be carefully considered before it is implemented. Another major component of the irrevocable trust that must be considered is the fact that an effective transfer to an irrevocable trust is a gift. Therefore, the trustor needs to examine the tax consequences of that gift and how the gift taxes are to be paid.

Domestic Versus Offshore

In creating a trust, the trustor must also decide whether to create an offshore trust or a domestic trust. This will depend upon the purpose(s) of the trust. A domestic trust is one created under the laws of one of the states in the United States of America. An offshore trust is one created under the laws of a foreign country, such as the Cayman Islands, the Cook Islands, or one of the many other foreign countries where these trusts can be created.

Using an offshore trust is very complicated. Any decision to establish such a trust should not be taken lightly, and anyone wanting to implement this form of planning should always seek expert professional help. There are many decisions to be made, beginning with where the foreign jurisdiction of the trust is to be, who are to be the offshore trustees, whether the trust is to be treated as a grantor trust and what assets are to be transferred to it. There are many IRS tax rules to be aware of and reporting obligations to be fulfilled. Offshore planning is not only expensive to set up, it is very expensive to maintain.

Offshore trusts are highly suspect by both the IRS and the legal community. In the past several years, litigation regarding these trusts has raised serious questions as to their validity as effective asset protection entities. We think there are better ways to protect assets both domestically and offshore than the offshore trust. One of these, for instance, might be a private annuity in conjunction with an international business corporation (IBC). In any event, the purpose for using such a trust should be carefully weighed, and the size of the assets to be placed offshore should be very substantial before the use of an offshore trust is even considered.

Privacy

One other important feature shared by most trusts is the privacy they can afford the trustor and the beneficiaries. While other entities, such as a corporation or limited partnership, must be registered with a state agency, there is no such requirement that a trust be registered. There is no compelling reason to record a trust so it becomes public knowledge. This means that unless the trustee voluntarily reveals information about the trust, no one can find out what assets are in the trust, the identity of the beneficiaries, or even if the trust exists. Thus, for purposes of privacy, using a trust can be advantageous.

Obviously the possibilities for providing for beneficiaries are endless. For this reason, trusts are very flexible and desirable tools. In the next chapter, we will continue the discussion of trusts, outlining those that have been designed for specific purposes.

CHAPTER 9

SPECIFIC TYPES OF TRUSTS

There are two fairly common types of trusts that bear discussion: irrevocable life insurance trusts and charitable remainder trusts. Both are extremely useful in the right situations. We will discuss the benefits of those types of trusts and touch on some types of trusts to be avoided.

IRREVOCABLE LIFE INSURANCE TRUSTS

Irrevocable life insurance trusts, or ILITs, are often used in conjunction with many other types of estate and business plans and are primarily used as asset replacement tools. In certain estate plans, ILITs are very beneficial. For example, ILITs may be the best option for some plans in which the assets are to be transferred to a third party, such as a charity, or in which the estate has inheritance tax liability. The ILIT is set up to hold an insurance policy that will replace the money or assets that have been given away or spent to cover taxes upon the death of the insured. An ILIT is also a good tool that can be used to protect insurance proceeds or cash values from creditors. It is not uncommon for ILITs to be used in conjunction with other trusts or with family-limited partnerships for a complete estate plan.

Life Policies

In the simplest situations, the ILIT is used to fund the projected tax liability of the estate. If this is to be the case, the amount of the tax to be paid is calculated based on the life expectancy of the taxpayer and the projected growth of the assets. Once the estimated dollar figure is established, a life insurance policy with a fixed amount of death benefit would be purchased to pay the estimated tax.

Different types of policies are available for this purpose. One of them is the last-to-die policy. A last-to-die policy only pays when the last beneficiary named in the policy dies. It is specifically designed for the use of spouses but is available to insure siblings or even other unrelated individuals. A complete discussion of all of the various policies available is outside the scope of this book and would detract from our focus. Suffice it to say that, ordinarily, a life insurance policy that generates a cash value is preferred because of the ability, at some point in time, to pay the premiums from the income earned on the cash value. We recommend consulting an insurance agent specializing in this area to work with your estate planning team to determine the appropriate amount and type of insurance for your particular situation.

Why Is a Trust Necessary?
Perhaps you are wondering why a trust is necessary at all. Why not just buy the insurance needed to cover the taxes and be done with it? Some insurance agents or investment advisors may counsel you to do that very thing. In fact, they may tell you the insurance proceeds will go to the beneficiary tax free. This is

true. However, what they fail to tell you is that if you pay for the policy, own the policy, or retain any incidents of ownership in the policy, the amount of the death benefit will be included in your estate for tax purposes. In other words, by paying for an insurance policy without establishing a trust, you increase your taxable estate, thereby adding to your original tax bill. This result can be avoided by creating a properly drafted life insurance trust to own the policy.

Incidence of Ownership

The irrevocable life insurance trust, true to its name, is irrevocable. Therefore, if the trust is to serve its intended purpose, the trustor must have no control over its assets. This means the trustee must be someone other than the trustor (or anyone closely related to him or her). Additionally, the trustor must not retain any control over the management of the trust, nor can the trustor reserve the right to change anything about the trust once it has been created. Obviously, the trustor cannot be the beneficiary of this trust. So usually, but not always, the spouse, the children, or the grandchildren are named as beneficiaries. These features of irrevocable trusts often discourage most people from using them. However, with respect to the irrevocable life insurance trust, the trustor is only placing the ownership of the life insurance policy in the trust, so the loss of control isn't a great problem. In addition, the ILIT offers an added benefit since the cash build-up in the policy will not be subject to the clutches of creditors.

The Three-Year Gift Rule

In some instances, the ILIT will be funded with the ownership of an insurance policy previously owned by the trustor. If this is the case, the gift of the existing policy will be subject to the "three-year gift rule." This rule simply means that if the donor/ trustor dies within three years of making the gift, the gifted property would still be taxable to the estate. The three-year gift rule applies to any transfer made within three years prior to death because such transfers are deemed to be "in contemplation of death." There are additional aspects related to gifting an existing insurance policy that are beyond the scope of this book. These components should be discussed with your estate planning team.

Premium Payments

Sometimes, the trustor will make a one-time gift of enough cash to pay the entire premium on a policy up front. This gift is made directly to the trustee of the trust and is then used by the trustee to purchase the policy. However, making a one-time gift is not always the most desirable way to cover the premium. For example, this isn't the best alternative if the premium is substantial enough to cause the donor to have a gift tax problem or an incident of ownership problem that would cause the proceeds of the policy to be included in the trustor's estate upon death. Ordinarily, the trustee is gifted the amount of the premium due each year. Even this, however, has been interpreted by the IRS as enough of an incident of ownership to include the face amount of the policy in the estate of the trustor. In such situations, attorneys are able to use the "Crummey powers" to avoid having the insurance policy included in the estate.

Crummey Powers

The name "Crummey", used in this context, does not mean undesirable. It is derived from a case in which Mr. and Mrs. Crummey wanted to make premium payments to their irrevocable life insurance trust; take the gift tax exclusion for the gift, and not have the policy value included in their estate. To accomplish this, the Crummeys made a gift of the premium amount to the trustee as a current gift to each of the beneficiaries. The trustee then had each of the beneficiaries sign a waiver releasing their respective share of the gift, and the trustee used those funds to pay the premiums on the insurance policy. The IRS said this was a proper method to avoid the inclusion rules and allowed the gift tax exclusion of up to $10,000 (currently $12,000) to each donor. By giving the gift to the beneficiaries first, it became a gift of a "present interest," and there was no incident of ownership when the funds were later used to pay the insurance premium.

The IRS did put some conditions on this transaction. One restriction requires that the beneficiaries actually receive a notice, which would contain notice of the gift and which would allow a reasonable time for them to respond. The beneficiaries also have to make a knowing waiver of their rights to actually receive the gift. Therefore, by using properly structured Crummey powers provisions and notice, it is possible to pay the premiums on an ongoing basis and use the annual gift tax exclusion to avoid the tax.

CHARITABLE REMAINDER TRUSTS

<u>In recent years charitable giving has become a popular way to avoid paying high capital gains tax on greatly appreciated property</u>, such as real estate and securities. A charitable remainder trust (CRT) can be a wonderful tool for those wanting to gift all or a portion of their assets during their lifetime. A charitable remainder trust has numerous tax advantages, can create great income benefits for the trustor, and provides asset protection from creditors as well. Some charitable institutions, especially hospitals and universities, have become quite aggressive in their solicitation of funds from this type of estate planning. In some instances, these institutions even offer to pay most of the attorney fees and costs for implementing these plans in order to be named as the charitable beneficiary.

A word of warning to would-be donors: Sometimes there are strings attached to the seeming generosity of a charitable organization offering estate planning help. We believe it is best if the person giving the gift chooses this type of estate planning based on a true charitable intent, rather than simply doing it to save taxes or attorney fees. A donor should always implement such a plan independently in order to avoid the conflicts of interest that could arise from having the charity unduly involved in the planning. Because this type of planning is sophisticated and sometimes confusing, an individual who wishes to set up a charitable remainder trust should use independent counsel in every case in order to gain a thorough understanding of all the issues involved.

The Trust

A charitable remainder trust must be irrevocable. However, unlike the ILIT, the charitable remainder trust can name the trustor as the trustee. A charitable remainder trust can also give the trustor, the trustor's children, and even the trustor's grandchildren, the life income generated in the trust. The remainder of the trust assets will go to a tax-qualified charity at the death of the last beneficiary. These trusts are generally used when there are non-income-producing (or under-income-producing) assets in the estate that are highly appreciated and would cost the trustor a large capital gains tax if they were sold outright.

How the Charitable Remainder Trust Works

In order for the charitable remainder trust to benefit the trustor, the type of property transferred to the trust (say, for instance, stocks or real estate) must be owned outright (free of liens or mortgages) and be readily saleable. Before transferring property to this type of trust, we recommend that the owner have some degree of certainty that the property can be sold for the desired price. Otherwise, the trustor could be in the position of having lost title to the property and receiving no income to boot. In addition to being fairly certain that the property can be sold, the property owner must refrain from entering into any type of legal agreement to actually sell the property before it is placed in the trust. Once the property has been transferred to the trust, the trustee will sell it and place the entire amount of the proceeds into income-producing investments for the benefit of the trustor. The amount of income paid to the beneficiary can be a set amount each year or a percentage of the earnings of the trust.

Asset Protection

Assuming there are no "fraudulent transfer" issues, once the asset has been transferred to the irrevocable trust, it is out of reach of the creditors of the trustor. However, an issue does arise regarding a creditor's right to the income received by the trustor. In most jurisdictions, the income received would be subject to a lien. However, it might be possible to structure the trust so that income would be payable to the spouse as separate property, in order to avoid any creditors. In any case, the income to any future lifetime beneficiaries would be safe from the trustor's creditors.

Privacy

As with other trusts, there is no need to publicly disclose the fact that a charitable remainder trust exists. However, in order to complete the gift, it would most likely be advisable to record the gift of any real property to the trust. Doing so establishes the existence of the trust as a matter of public record and substantiates the gift for IRS tax purposes. This portion of the transaction would then become visible. However, the exact terms of the trust agreement itself would not be available to scrutiny.

Tax Advantages

This charitable remainder trust arrangement allows the trustor to sell the property without paying any capital gains tax because the property is now owned by the charitable trust, which doesn't pay tax. In addition to not paying taxes on the proceeds from the sale, selling the property increases the trustor's income by allowing reinvesting of the sale proceeds, because without the tax there is more money to invest through the charitable remainder trust. The trustor is also able to claim the transfer of the property as a charitable gift and take an income tax deduction. Very nice arrangement, wouldn't you say?

The only drawback to this arrangement is that the children of the trustor will not inherit the property. The charity inherits it. Children, however, and even grandchildren if they are born at the time of the gift, can be entitled to income from the trust for their lifetimes if the trustor so desires. So what are the children really losing? Actually, they may be losing a lot, considering the cost of inflation and the possibility of appreciation of the property over a lengthy time period.

By giving away a portion of the estate to a charity, the donors have not used any of their estate tax exemption. They have removed that property from their estate entirely because they no longer own it. Now they will be able, under current law, to leave their heirs an estate worth up to $4 million (for a married couple) or $2 million (for a single individual) tax free. Taking this into consideration, the children may still come out ahead. Additionally, there may be another way the children can have their cake and eat it too. This is where the ILIT, previously discussed, can come into play. Let's see how that can work.

Why couldn't the trustors buy life insurance that would pay the children the amount of money they would have inherited had the property not been given to the charity? That could be a solution. However, with this option the proceeds would have to be included in the gross estate for tax purposes, and there would be tax due upon the trustor's death. How about an irrevocable life insurance trust? An ILIT would avoid the estate tax, and the proceeds of the insurance wouldn't be taxable to the children either. They could then receive cash in place of the property and enjoy the income from the trust as well. Assuming the trustors are insurable, the insurance premiums could be paid with the extra income earned from the capital gains tax savings and the tax savings created by the gift to the charity. As you can see, in the right situation, this type of planning can be extremely advantageous.

TRUSTS TO AVOID

In this chapter, we have outlined the benefits of certain trusts. However, some trusts should be avoided at all costs because they can lead to serious trouble with the law or taxing authorities. Trusts to steer clear of include those known as a "constitutional trust," "pure trust," or "constitutional business organization." Promoters of these shady plans claim that such trusts avoid all taxes, protect against creditors, and avoid probate. However, these trusts don't provide any of these benefits. They have legitimacy and jurisdictional problems. Our advice is to avoid them like the plague. They are scams and will only cause you grief with the IRS. Further information about these trusts can be acquired from your estate planning attorney.

CHAPTER 10

REVOCABLE LIVING TRUSTS

Since the early 1980s, the revocable living trust has risen to the forefront of estate planning and become the document of choice. Because of its benefits, we predict that the revocable living trust will be the most popular estate planning tool in the new millennium.

History of the Modern Living Trust

Until recently, most planned estates used the last will and testament as the primary centerpiece for estate planning. For most estates, wills were thought to be the only way to plan. Wills were simple and could be prepared by almost any attorney. However, they also had a major drawback. With a will, an estate automatically went to probate court, where it was subject to the lengthy and expensive probate process. In an attempt to avoid probate, people began looking for alternatives that would deliver their estate from this consequence. Then a new development, quite unprecedented in legal circles, had a dramatic and explosive impact in the estate planning arena. In early 1984, as the widespread use of the computer started to take hold, a different way of estate planning, the revocable living trust, began to be offered to the general public.

Actually, the revocable living trust was not new at all. This type of trust had been around for hundreds of years and was first known to be used by English lords to escape the taxes imposed by the king. These nobles discovered that by placing title to their property in the hands of the Church "in trust" for their own use and benefit, they were in the unique position of being able to escape the taxes levied by the king on that particular property. Once a lord transferred the legal title to the property to the Church, he no longer legally owned the property. (The Church owned it, and the Church was exempt from paying property taxes.)

Because the trust was revocable (it could be voided any time the lord wished), he was in an enviable position. The lord no longer owned the property and didn't have to pay taxes on it. Yet, he still had total control over its use and received its benefits. Under this arrangement, the Church also benefited because the Church collected a fee from the lord for this service. Further, when the lord died, he didn't risk having his heirs disinherited by the king since the Church retained legal title to the property and had promised to substitute the Lord's heirs as the beneficial owners. This was an attractive arrangement for everybody except the king. As the years passed, these revocable trusts continued to be used by the wealthy to minimize taxes, particularly taxes on inheritances, and to keep the wealth of the family intact for successive generations.

Revocable living trusts have been used in the United States since the country's founding. However, since revocable living trusts are quite lengthy documents and, until recently, were costly to prepare, only the very rich could afford them. This began to change in the mid-1980s as the use of electronic word processing machines and personal computers made lengthy document preparation easier and far less expensive. At that time, a few far-sighted attorneys saw the value of using this type of trust document for smaller estates as a way of avoiding probate.

<u>A revocable living trust is an excellent alternative to the last will and testament.</u> In the way it is most popularly used, the name "living trust" is a misnomer. In actuality, a living trust is simply a trust created by a person during his or her lifetime, and there are many types of living trusts. However, the name living trust has taken on its own meaning and interpretation. While the shorter phrase living trust means any living trust, it is commonly used when referring specifically to the revocable living trust.

Once this new trend began it suddenly seemed everyone was selling living trusts, as though one size fits all. Financial planners, accountants, insurance agents, and stockbrokers all got into the act, presenting workshops and seminars on living trusts. Even many reputable law firms got into the business of "pushing trusts." Instead of counseling and planning with their clients, these professionals were cranking out living trusts for ridiculously low prices, and at those prices, competent legal counseling wasn't economically feasible.

In many cases, clients were paying for nothing more than formula word processing, and often there was some secondary motive involved in these sales. Frequently, the trust was a hook, and the true objective was to sell annuities or other financial products to unsuspecting clients. As a general rule, these trust peddlers were completely untrained in the legalities of such trusts, and they operated under the guise that competent legal counsel wasn't required. While these incidents have decreased, such practices continue today with many self-proclaimed trust experts churning out living trusts and, in some cases, charging exorbitant fees and producing work that is not only shoddy but often not even legally binding.

If we seem to belabor this discussion, it's because we feel so strongly about the misuse of what can be a fantastic estate planning tool. Even though some of this abuse has died down, it is still going on across the country. The California State Bar and other state legislatures are now holding hearings designed to stop this type of illegal activity. They consider much of the activity surrounding the sale of living trusts to be practicing law without a license, and it has been prosecuted as a criminal offense. To date, at least one large company operating in California has been criminally prosecuted and is presently facing a multitude of civil lawsuits.

In order to enjoy the desired results, a revocable living trust must be professionally and competently planned, and that requires the skills of your entire estate planning team. It can be beneficial, however, to use a software program on revocable living trusts to help prepare your estate plan before you see your attorney. This will clarify the issues for discussion and save time and money.

In the first few years of their popularity, living trusts caused a major uproar within the legal community. Many conservative lawyers resisted its use and tried to downplay the benefits of the living trust, doggedly advocating the use of a will instead. However, they simply could not overcome the obvious major benefit of the trust—the avoidance of probate. Today, much has changed. The legal community is now solidly in favor of the use of the living trust, and experts in the field have devised and discovered many new ways to beneficially use these very flexible documents.

We wholeheartedly advocate the revocable living trust and believe it should be the centerpiece of everyone's estate plan. If before reading this book you thought you just needed a will, chances are what you really need is a living trust. We know that, even with all of the publicity received by living trusts in the last few years, many people still have not heard about living trusts or have not received enough information to form an opinion or may have even formed some misconceptions about living trusts. In the next few sections, we will outline some of the most important issues regarding what has become our favorite estate planning tool.

WHAT IS A LIVING TRUST?

A living trust is commonly presented as a portfolio of legal documents, which includes a "trust agreement" or a "declaration of trust" as the main document. The living trust is designed to be a full estate plan, which not only takes care of issues that arise upon the death of the maker of the trust (trustor) but also addresses many issues that come into play during the maker's lifetime. The complete living trust portfolio also contains several other documents, which will be discussed in greater detail later in this chapter. These documents include a pour-over will, a financial durable power of attorney, a health care durable power of attorney, a physician's directive preventing prolonged artificial life support, specific instructions to the trustee, and all the appropriate property transfer documents.

The trust agreement itself is the most important document in the portfolio and will receive the majority of our attention. The trust agreement is simply a lengthy contract between the maker or owner of the trust (the trustor) and the manager of the trust (the trustee). The provisions of the trust agreement spell out what assets are to be put into the trust, who the beneficiaries of the trust are to be, and how the trustee is to manage and distribute the assets to those beneficiaries. You most likely remember much of this from the previous discussion of trusts in general.

Revocable living trusts almost always name the owner (trustor) to serve in all three of the trust positions referred to above (trustor, trustee, and beneficiary). This means that during his or her lifetime, the trustor is also the trustee (manager of the trust) and the beneficiary. Remember that a living trust is revocable and amendable, and the trustor retains total control over the assets and transfers only bare legal title to the trustee. Due to its revocable nature, the trust is not required to file a tax return as a separate entity. The trustor simply continues to file a 1040 individual return under his or her Social Security number. No adverse tax consequences result from transferring property to this type of trust. <u>A revocable living trust is simple to create, very economical to maintain, and easy to manage and to use</u>.

Revocable living trusts only require periodic updates every few years. The flip side is that there is little asset protection or tax benefit to the trustor in entering into this trust arrangement.

WHAT'S SO GREAT ABOUT LIVING TRUSTS?

Avoids Probate

Avoiding probate is, in and of itself, a worthy endeavor. Probate is the legal process required to transfer the estate to the heirs of the deceased. Handled by the state court system, it is almost always a long, drawn-out, frustrating, and confusing affair. The process is extremely costly to the estate in terms of attorney and executor fees. Even more devastating is the time this process takes and the emotional toll on the heirs, who find themselves mired in legal muck when they are already suffering the loss of their loved one. Almost anyone who goes through this process will testify that it should be avoided. We highly recommend the revocable living trust as the best alternative to avoid probate.

Probate, as you remember, is a public procedure. Before distribution of the estate, the personal representative is required to publish notice of the decedent's demise and allow time for all creditors and claimants to file their claims with the probate court. Probate provides a grand opportunity for disgruntled relatives to get into the act. Not only that, the probate records are open to the public, which means the whole world can find out what assets are in the estate and who the beneficiaries are. That is very valuable for people who may want to gather information that could be used against the beneficiaries of such estates.

The Trust Provides One Place for All the Assets of the Estate

Having one pot which holds all of the estate assets for purposes of evaluation and distribution is highly desirable. Since assets are all in one place during the holding period of the trust, as the assets grow or fail to grow as the case may be, the effect is equal for all of the beneficiaries who are to receive a portion of the trust estate. Additionally, the expenses of the estate can be paid from the trust prior to distribution so all of the beneficiaries share equally in that burden.

Sometimes people make the mistake of setting up several individual stock accounts, annuities, CDs, or bank accounts and then naming different individuals as the beneficiaries on each of these accounts. For example, parents may set up individual accounts, each naming one of their children as the beneficiary. Over time, however, there can be considerable variance in the performance of these various accounts, which may result in a very unequal distribution to the beneficiaries. Also it may severely affect the other beneficiaries (heirs of the remainder of the estate) since other assets may be subject to creditors demands, expenses of administration, and taxes.

Such problems do not arise when all the assets are placed in the trust and accumulated for distribution there. By placing all of the assets in the trust, the trustee will have control of all of the assets to be distributed rather than having certain assets going to certain beneficiaries through beneficiary designations. The result of placing all the assets in this trust is continuity and equality in the distribution of the estate. No matter how a particular asset may have performed over a period of time, all of the assets are added together in one pot. Thus, an equal distribution can be made to each of the beneficiaries, if that is the intent of the trustor.

Conservatorship

The revocable living trust is a valuable estate planning tool in other respects as well. The living trust can facilitate the management of the estate if the trustor becomes incapacitated during his or her lifetime. If this were to occur, because all the assets are owned by the trust, a person appointed by the trustor to take over_the successor trustee_would manage the affairs of the trust during the trustor's disability. In such a situation, having a successor trustee designated in the trust means there is no need for a conservator to be appointed by a probate judge.

Conservatorship places the court in total control of the incapacitated person's monetary assets and his or her physical person. Under conservatorship, the court makes decisions regarding both the physical and financial health of that person. Additionally, conservatorship imposes extensive requirements that the person appointed as conservator continually report and prove that he or she is acting in the best interest of the incapacitated person. All of this expense is avoided by using a living trust.

Privacy

As with any trust, privacy is one of the key benefits of using the revocable living trust. In fact, a living trust has a unique feature that most other trusts do not have, making it even more attractive to those seeking privacy. The assets of a revocable living trust are treated as though they are still the assets of the trustor(s). That being the case, the income of the trust is not taxed to the trust, and the trust is not required to file a tax return. Because it is revocable, the IRS does not consider it an independent tax-paying entity until the death of the trustor(s) or until the trust is split into one or more trusts upon the death of the first spouse. Unlike other entities (such as corporations, limited liability companies, limited partnerships), a living trust is not required to register or to file with any agency. In most jurisdictions, the trust never becomes public knowledge unless the trustor wishes to record it for some reason.

Tax Considerations

For married persons, the revocable living trust provides substantial tax savings. However, the trust must be properly structured so it will split into two or more sub-trusts at the death of the first trustor. This arrangement accomplishes two specific goals. First, it gives the deceased person significant control over the estate, even after he or she passes on. Second, under current law, it allows the estate to shelter $4 million from federal inheritance tax. This is a savings of approximately $820,000 over that afforded by more traditional types of estate planning.

The revocable living trust offers other tax benefits. Transfers of real property to this type of trust do not cause reassessment of property for tax purposes. There is no realized taxable capital gain on transferred securities or other types of appreciated assets when they are transferred to the trust. Because the trust is revocable by the trustors during their lifetime, the trust is ignored for income tax purposes during the lifetime of the trustors. Better yet, the beneficiaries will receive a full step-up in cost-basis on the trust property at the time of the death of the last trustor, just as though the property had never been held in trust.

Asset Protection

While the living trust will not ordinarily protect the trustors' assets from the claims of their own creditors, it can protect the assets from an onslaught of claims from the heirs' creditors, so long as the assets remain in the trust. In addition, because the decedent's trust becomes irrevocable upon the death of the first spouse to die, it is possible to shield the assets in that trust from the creditors of the surviving spouse. With revocable living trusts, if the appropriate provisions are in place, the trust can become irrevocable if a trustor becomes incompetent. This, in some instances, protects the trust assets from creditors of the incompetent trustor.

Asset Control

One of the major advantages of the revocable living trust is that it leaves the trustor in complete control over the trust assets during his or her lifetime. The provisions of the revocable trust can be amended at any time, changing the allocation of those assets. Also, the trustors may move property in or out of the trust as they so desire. The trustors have complete authority over who is to take control of the revocable trust upon their death, who is to be the beneficiary or beneficiaries of the trust, and when and how the beneficiaries are to receive the trust benefits. This makes the living trust an ideal tool for families with minor children, or other dependents not legally able to fend for themselves. Young families would be wise to explore this option and carefully weigh its importance as a way of protecting the future of their minor children.

Living Trusts Are Easy to Create and Maintain

Any professional estate planning attorney can draft a revocable living trust. It is much less expensive to set up a living trust than it is to go the alternative route, which is to have the estate go through probate. Probate will often cost as much as 10 percent or more of the entire estate ($40,000 on a modest estate of $400,000). A living trust will cost, at most, $2,000-$3,000 even if the estate is complicated. With a living trust, maintenance is also inexpensive. A trust should be reviewed, preferably by the attorney who prepared it, at least every three years and/or whenever a major change occurs. (A major change is defined as a birth, death, divorce, remarriage, or other life-changing event for any of the beneficiaries.) The three-year review is suggested because, as in every other legal sphere where change is a constant occurrence, the laws regarding trusts do change from time to time. A trust should be kept current and should take legal advantage of any new benefits that may arise. Many estate planning attorneys are now offering their clients yearly maintenance programs at reduced fees for this purpose.

ANCILLARY DOCUMENTS

A properly prepared revocable living trust is the centerpiece of the estate plan and the actual trust document should always be accompanied by several other important documents, which coordinate with the trust and complete the estate plan. These documents include a Pour-Over Will, a financial Durable

Power of Attorney, a health care Durable Power of Attorney and a Physician's Directive.

Pour-Over Will

A well-designed plan will include an ancillary document commonly referred to as a pour-over will. This document is the last will and testament of the trustor, which by its terms leaves everything to the trustee of the trust. In other words, it "pours the assets over into the trust." Hence, it's name.

The purpose of this will is to back up the trust by leaving any assets that were not titled to the trust at the death of the trustor to the trustee so that they can be distributed along with all of the other assets. However, this procedure does not avoid probate if the assets outside the trust exceed the threshold for probate in the state where the trustor resides at the time of death.

For example, in California the threshold to probate is $100,000. Assets totaling less than that do not have to be formally probated unless they are real property. In California, real property valued at more than $20,000 is subject to probate. Thus, if $99,000 worth of personal property assets were not titled to the trust at the time of death, they would be transferred to the trustee by a simple affidavit procedure and avoid probate. This would be partly accomplished by utilizing the provision of the pour-over will. We feel the best practice is to never intentionally leave assets outside the trust. You thus avoid running into the probate rules in your state.

Powers of Attorney

A well-designed plan will also include two powers of attorney. Powers of attorney are agreements between two or more people wherein one person (the principal) gives power to the other person (the agent) to act for him. This can be for only specific acts, such as selling a certain parcel of real estate (a limited power of attorney), or to act in all matters pertaining to the principal's financial affairs (a general power of attorney).

Powers of attorney can be designed for many different purposes and can vary greatly in their terms. Some powers deal with financial matters and others deal with the health care of the principal. All of them expire upon the death of the principal. Some states now have what is known as "true durables," which are powers of attorney that last for the life of the principal. Other states have powers of attorney that often last for five to seven years from the date of signature. In either case, it is important that your trust portfolio include at least the following two durable powers.

Durable Power of Attorney over Assets

A durable power of attorney over assets is an important backup document to the trust. If the trustor were to become mentally incompetent or unable to sign his or her name for any reason, this document would give the appointed agent the authority to sign the trustor's name and to transfer assets to the trust or to even create a trust. Then, once the asset is in the trust, the acting trustee manages it on behalf of the trustor/beneficiary.

In most cases, the authority of the agent doesn't arise until such time as two licensed physicians have declared the trustor incompetent. This is called a "springing power of attorney" because it only comes into effect on the occurrence of certain events, such as declared incompetence, and will only be valid during such period of disability. This springing power is the power that is most often used since many people are not comfortable with signing a general power of attorney that is immediately enforceable under any circumstances.

Durable Power of Attorney over Health Care

Even though it doesn't directly deal with the material assets of the trust, the durable power of attorney over health care is a critical document that is normally included in the estate plan portfolio. This document works much like the durable power over assets except that it gives authority to another person to make health care decisions for the trustor in the event he or she becomes unable to make such decisions.

Like the power of attorney over assets, the power to make health care decisions does not arise unless the trustor/principal has been certified by a licensed physician as unable to act for himself or herself. This powerful document, in most instances, even gives the agent the power to direct that the trustor be taken off life-support devices. Because this is a great responsibility, the agent is bound by law in many states to follow exactly the wishes of the principal in respect to health care. In order to ensure the principal's wishes are adhered to, a document entitled a "physician's directive" is often used in conjunction with this power of attorney.

Physician's Directive

The physician's directive is a legal document more commonly known as the "living will." The purpose of this directive is to define the trustor's wishes regarding all aspects of medical treatment, particularly life-support issues. Often, this document is designed to tell physicians and hospital staff that the person signing the document does not want heroic efforts made to prolong life, especially if he or she has fallen into a vegetative state and has no quality of life remaining. The idea is to prevent the estate from being depleted due to expensive medical procedures, which will not likely result in any lasting benefits to the patient. People who sign this type of document would rather preserve their wealth for their family than make their physicians wealthy.

LIVING TRUSTS ARE FOR EVERYONE

For the many reasons explained in this chapter, plus the psychological and emotional benefits a revocable living trust affords the heirs, we strongly recommend this type of estate planning. A revocable living trust is suggested for any person who owns any real property and/or has other assets valued above the amount that would put your estate into probate based on the guidelines for your state. You can easily find out what your state's limit is by calling the probate court in your city or county. Often the amount is very low. In one state, for example, estates of only $3,000 are subject to probate. In that state, if an individual has nothing more than a car that runs, the car alone would be enough to put the estate over the probate limit.

COMPARISON CHART

THIS CHART LISTS ATTRIBUTES THAT ARE CHARACTERISTIC OF THE ESTATE PLANNING TOOL, WHICH HEADS THE CATEGORY. FOR EXAMPLE, WHETHER YOU HAVE A WILL OR NOT, YOU COULD BE SUBJECT TO PROBATE OR CONSERVATORSHIP, BUT, IF YOU HAVE A LIVING TRUST, YOU WILL NOT BE SUBJECT TO THESE PROCESSES.

	NO WILL	WILL	LIVING TRUST	GIFT	JOINT TENANT
CONSERVATORSHIP	X	X	NO	N/A	X
PROBATE	X	X	NO	N/A	
CONTROL		X	X		
FLEXIBILITY		X	X		
PRIVACY			X		
FAIR DISTRIBUTIONS		X	X	X	
DIFFICULT TO CONTEST			X	X	X
PRE-NUPTIAL BENEFITS			X		
TAX REDUCTION		X	X	X	
ASSET MANAGEMENT			X		
PEACE OF MIND			X		

CHAPTER 11

CHOOSING YOUR TRUSTEE

In your efforts to leave behind a perfect last impression, the trustee you choose to oversee your trust can become your greatest aid or your worst nightmare. Which person should you choose to act in this capacity and why? The choice will depend, in part, on how your trust is to be structured, who the beneficiaries are to be, and how the trust property is to be distributed. In addition, a trustor must also focus on how the choice of the trustee can assist or detract from the ultimate goal—accurately communicating the trustor's desired final message.

First, a few comments regarding larger estates, and then we'll move to considerations that apply to every case.

Larger Estates

With larger estates, complicated legal and tax-related issues are often involved, and in many cases, the trust property is to be held for a long period of time so as to benefit future generations. Therefore, choosing a trustee for a larger estate is more complex than selecting a trustee for a smaller estate where there is to be an immediate distribution of all the property to the heirs after the trustor's death.

When long-term management obligations are imposed upon the trustee, in addition to the investment and accounting criteria that must be legally met, certain issues become of critical importance. A trustor would want to consider the potential trustee's history of investment experience, as well as the individual's personal health and who would replace the trustee in the event of his or her death. For trusts in which long-term service or specialized knowledge is required, it may be advisable for the trustor to consider appointing both a personal and a corporate trustee to act as co-trustees. The personal trustee can conduct the day-to-day relations with the beneficiaries, and the corporate trustee can fulfill the investment and reporting requirements in a manner consistent with both the law and the trustor's expectations.

By assigning both a personal trustee and a corporate trustee, a trustor creates a best-of-both-worlds scenario because the personal trustee can address the concerns of the beneficiaries and the legal obligations of administering the trust can be handled by the corporate trustee. Having co-trustees also means that if the personal trustee should die, the administration of the trust can continue with little interruption. The corporate trustee would continue unchanged until a new personal trustee was appointed.

Another case in which the appointment of a corporate co-trustee is a good idea is in the event that a surviving spouse is to be the trustee and life beneficiary of the trust. By appointing a corporate trustee, the spouse is afforded good asset protection with regard to assets in the spouse's trust because the surviving spouse would not have absolute control over the distribution of the principal. At the same time, the use of co-trustees protects the children (or other beneficiaries) because it controls the use of the principal of the trust. Such an arrangement is especially desirable when children of a prior marriage are involved or when liability to creditors might be a concern.

Remember, you always have the option of appointing co-trustees to administer or settle a trust, and it is not always necessary to name a corporate trustee as one of the co-trustees. Personal trustees may also serve together as co-trustees, especially if one of the personal trustees has extensive investment experience.

PERSONAL TRUSTEES VS. INSTITUTIONAL (CORPORATE) TRUSTEES

Personal trustees can be family members, friends, business associates or professionals, such as attorneys, accountants, or financial consultants. Institutional (or corporate) trustees have traditionally been licensed trust companies and banks. Recently, brokerage houses, such as Salomon Smith Barney, A.G. Edwards, and others, have entered this field.

There is much controversy among estate planning professionals as to the benefits of using a personal trustee, a corporate trustee, or both. Institutional trustees are viewed as more reliable for several reasons. They often have an established track record in handling such matters, and corporate trustees are financially accountable in the event that they do cause financial damage to the beneficiaries of the trust. Finally, corporate trustees have a perpetual lifetime because a corporate trustee does not die.

On the other hand, institutional (corporate) trustees may have a number of drawbacks. They can be insensitive to the personal needs of the beneficiaries, and they are usually slow to move on unusual or discretionary decisions. Further, institutional trustees are often accused of taking an approach that is too conservative when it comes to investing the trust assets, and, thus, limiting the trust's income and growth potential. It will be interesting to see how the brokerage houses handle this aspect of trusteeship and equally interesting to see how the 1998 Uniform Prudent Investor Act affects investment performance by institutional trustees.

The Uniform Laws, one of which is the Uniform Prudent Investors Act, are laws promulgated by a national group made up of attorneys from each state. This group creates adoptive legislation affecting issues that are of national concern and for which some semblance of agreement among the states is felt to be of major importance. Since this group, known as the National Conference of Commissioners of Uniform State Law, is a nongovernmental body, these laws are only enforceable in the states that do adopt them either in whole or in part. To date, a majority of the states have adopted the Uniform Prudent Investor Act in some form. Information about this act should be available by researching the probate codes of the state in question or from an estate planning attorney practicing in that particular jurisdiction. Where such laws are in effect, trustees are legally obligated to abide by them.

<u>Personal trustees</u>—whether they are family members, friends, or business associates—<u>are viewed as much more sensitive to the needs of the beneficiaries</u>. They usually have more personal knowledge of the family and its affairs and are more loving and more personally involved. Personal trustees are seen as using more good common sense. On the other hand, family or friends often do not have a proven track record with handling estate planning matters. They may be indecisive or insecure about investment or business decisions, and they may be prejudiced toward certain beneficiaries. Business associates and professionals may have good business or investment skills but may be too involved with other business matters to do a good job as a trustee. Personal trustees may be more apt to speculate in risky deals or to embezzle funds than a corporate trustee would be, since personal trustees are not usually financially accountable for damage caused to the beneficiaries as a result of their mistakes or misconduct. All of these potential drawbacks must be weighed in light of the purpose for selecting the trustee and the complexity of the situation.

Usually, if the estate is not extremely large and the issues are not complex, trustors avoid appointing institutional trustees. On the other hand, trusts with more complex issues and with ongoing management needs often call for a corporate trustee. In many cases, estates that require ongoing investment decisions or that have a large amount of assets to be handled would be best served by having both a personal and corporate trustee to serve as a counterbalance to one another. When making this decision, it is best to discuss your overall needs and objectives with your estate planning attorney.

Considerations Applicable to Every Case

<u>Every trust must have a trustee who manages the assets of the trust</u>. The trustor of a revocable living trust also commonly serves as the initial trustee. In drafting the trust, the trustor names a person(s) who will act as successor trustee. The successor trustee will take the initial trustee's place when one of three events occurs: when the last trustor dies, when the last trustor is incapacitated or declared incompetent, or when the last trustor no longer desires to manage the trust assets and resigns. The successor trustee's job is to take the place of the initial trustee and to manage the assets in the best interest of the beneficiaries of the trust.

Most often, the successor trustee steps in upon the death of the last trustor. We say the last trustor, because, in a marital trust, when one spouse dies, the other spouse becomes the sole trustee. However, the surviving spouse is not a successor trustee, since he or she was an initial trustee. In many cases, perhaps most cases, the successor trustee is one of the children of the trustor.

In the majority of cases where there is to be immediate settlement of the trust upon the death of the last trustor, a personal trustee can adequately handle the situation with the guidance and help of the estate planning attorney. Usually, a family member or trusted friend is willing to act in this capacity. The key words are "willing to act," since the duties of a trustee are many and must be taken seriously. The trustee acts as a fiduciary to the beneficiaries. This means the trustee must act in a manner that is in the best interest of the beneficiaries and that is above reproach in carrying out the instructions given by the trustor in the trust agreement.

If there are minor children, we suggest using co-trustees, as discussed previously, in order to achieve greater protection of the children's interests. A corporate trustee (or an investment-experienced personal trustee) would manage the investments, and a personal trustee would see to the children's personal needs. This arrangement works well as it gives the guardian of the children (who may or may not be the same person as the personal trustee) the opportunity to work with the financial trustee and to advise the trustee of the children's needs.

Another question arises: Who looks over the shoulder of the successor trustee to see that he or she is acting appropriately and in the best interest of the beneficiaries? The beneficiaries police the actions of the trustee and take legal action if the trustee is neglecting his or her duties or is otherwise mishandling the trust assets. This being the case, it is always advisable to consider the personalities involved when choosing the personal trustee to handle your family trust. Does the potential trustee get along with the other beneficiaries, or will he or she be overbearing and unpleasant? Have there been any long-standing hard feelings among any of the beneficiaries and this person? If so, how can you defuse this situation? Will the person you choose be inclined to play favorites among the family members or any of the other beneficiaries? Will this person willingly follow your instructions? Will this person be assertive enough to handle other strong-willed beneficiaries? These considerations are all important, since your personal trustee will play a key role in helping to communicate your final message to your heirs.

Since the beneficiaries protect their own interests by monitoring the trustee's behavior, it is important to make sure that the beneficiaries, under reasonable circumstances, have some way of replacing the trustee. Including a provision that allows beneficiaries to replace a trustee may prevent the necessity for legal proceedings. The beneficiaries can always use the courts for help in protecting their rights, but court proceedings are both time-consuming and expensive and should be the last resort. All of the provisions regarding the appointment of the successor trustee, the replacement of the trustee, and the rights of the beneficiary and/or trustor should be clearly and adequately spelled out in the trust document.

Duties of a Trustee

In times past, a trustee was expected to act as would "a reasonable man in the same or similar circumstances." However, that standard is no longer adequate. Today, the trustee is held to an even higher standard, particularly when investment of trust assets for any period of time is involved. Today, a trustee needs to be familiar with the Uniform Prudent Investor Act and is expected to have expertise as an investor or to hire an advisor who does have such expertise.

What are the duties of the trustee? The trustee's first and most important job is to follow the instructions given to him by the trustor. These instructions are laid out in the provisions of the trust agreement.

In cases where the trust is to be settled and distributed upon the death of the trustor, the trustee's initial job is to value all the items of personal property that the trustors have indicated should go to particular beneficiaries. Once valued, the trustee will distribute the items to the appropriate person. The next duty of the trustee is to "marshal the remaining assets of the trust." That means the trustee will demand payment of all life insurance policies and annuities and transfer all other bank accounts to the trust settlement account and transfer CD funds, bonds and stocks to the trust account. The trustee will also take control over IRAs or other tax-deferred property and will appraise or sell all real property or personal property held by the trust that isn't otherwise specifically disposed of by the trustors. If there are assets outside of the trust to be distributed to the trust by virtue of a pour-over will, the trustee will take care of those transfers as well. For estate tax purposes, the trustee must also list all other property outside the trust that goes to other beneficiaries through joint tenancy or beneficiary designation.

Next, the trustee must see that any tax returns required to be filed by the trustor or the estate are properly prepared and filed. All obligations owed by the estate, including taxes, must be paid. Then, the trustee must prepare an accounting to each of the beneficiaries, along with distribution of their respective portions of the trust. Often, it is advisable for the trustee to hold a small amount of trust funds for a period of time to be sure that funds are available to pay any creditors or liabilities owed by the estate that might come to light later. Without such retention, the trustee would have to attempt to get money back from the beneficiaries to pay expenses that were later identified. If unsuccessful, the trustee could be in a position of having to pay for these expenses personally. It isn't easy and can be quite time-consuming for a trustee to accomplish all the activities of even a simple estate transfer. In more complex cases, many more details must be attended to.

While the trustee is taking care of the many aspects of the distribution of the trust, he or she must also deal with the beneficiaries. According to some states' requirements, the trustee must properly notify the beneficiaries of their rights to have copies of the trust and of the legal timeframes in which they may challenge the trust provisions. In other words, it is the trustee who generally keeps the beneficiaries informed as to the progress of the settlement. The trustee may hire a professional, such as an estate planning attorney or an accountant, to assist in these matters.

Trustee Payment

What payment does the trustee receive? Even if the trust fails to specify payment, the trustee is entitled to reasonable fees for his or her services. In most cases, institutional trustees will require that compensation be agreed upon before they undertake the task. Institutional trustees commonly have a fee schedule, which spells out trustee fees. These schedules are usually on a sliding scale (as the value of the trust assets goes up, the percentage amount charged is reduced). These fees tend to be fairly uniform throughout the industry and usually start at about two percent (2%) of the total assets, paid on an annual basis. (Many institutional trustees will not handle estates valued at less than $500,000.)

Personal trustees are also entitled to reasonable fees, based on court schedules or on fees comparable to what an institutional trustee would charge. Sometimes, family members will waive their right to fees. However, it is our experience that with the amount of work a trustee must do, he really does deserve to be paid. We believe, in most instances, personal trustees are sorely underpaid for all the time and effort they expend in settling an estate.

Importance of the Trustee

Carefully choosing a trustee is critical. This one decision will greatly affect the kind of last impression you leave with your heirs. One of the most important things that must be considered is whether the trustee is emotionally capable of dealing with the other beneficiaries in a fair and objective way. Even the best plan, which appears to be fair and seems to be agreed to by all parties, could easily go awry if the wrong trustee is chosen to carry it out.

Joe's story shows the effect that the wrong trustee can have on an otherwise fairly good estate plan. Joe's mother, Dorothy, who lived in another state, was very ill and did not have long to live. Joe took a leave of absence from his job and traveled to see his mother. He stayed with her for almost two months before she died. Joe's sister, Jan, had always lived near their mother and had been her primary caretaker for the last few years. Joe's brother, Pete, also lived out of the state but, like Joe, came to be with Dorothy during her last illness. While Jan had always been friendly with both brothers, Pete and Joe had been estranged for several years. Dorothy's illness now brought them closer together again. Financially, both brothers were barely scraping by; Jan and her husband were well off.

While all of the children were there, Dorothy told them that, at Jan's insistence, she had made a living trust and she was leaving her house and all of its contents to her daughter as repayment for all of the time Jan had spent as caretaker. Mom did not want this to cause any dissension, and she asked for their opinions. She expressed how much she loved each one and that her fondest wish was for her children to have a warm and loving relationship among themselves when she was gone. She told them she had prayed that they would all be together again, and she was thrilled that all three of her children could be with her at this time.

The house was the major asset in the trust. Dorothy had owned an automobile, but after she could no longer drive, she had given it to one of Jan's children. In addition to the house, there were some bank and savings accounts to be divided. Twenty percent was to go to Jan, with the balance divided equally between the sons. The understanding between Dorothy and her children was that Jan would use the 20 percent to pay any expenses that might be due after Dorothy was gone.

Both men thought Dorothy's decision was fair and felt Jan deserved this additional compensation. As Dorothy's illness became worse, Jan began to make it clear more and more that she was in charge and that her brothers had no say about their mother's care. This began to cause problems and resentments among the three children but, thinking Dorothy was too ill to worry about it, none of them said anything to their mother. Both brothers were astonished that Jan's attitude became increasingly bossy and controlling as their mother's health declined, but Joe was particularly disturbed as he often disagreed with Jan's decisions regarding their mother's care.

When Dorothy finally passed away, Jan informed her brothers that, as trustee of the trust, she was in charge of everything. She made all of the burial arrangements without consulting with her brothers. She refused to give either brother a copy of their mother's trust. She then hired an attorney and refused to have any further direct communication with either of the brothers. Jan held the trust open and paid all of the ongoing household expenses from the trust funds. She even went so far as to use trust funds to make home improvements so she would get a better price for the sale of the house.

When the house sold, Jan distributed the proceeds of the sale to herself without repaying the trust any of the money she had spent for maintenance, repairs, or improvements. After paying all the expenses, including taxes owed, Jan divided the small amount that was left—20 percent to herself and the balance divided equally between her brothers. The brothers were livid at Jan's selfish and unfair handling of the trust but did not feel they could afford the legal fees to contest her actions. The brothers have cut off any contact with Jan, and the chance of the three of them ever having a close relationship has most likely been lost.

In this case, Dorothy's estate included a house, furnishings, and automobile, which were valued at about $350,000. In addition, there was about $40,000 in the bank. Jan not only got the house, furniture, and car, but she also paid all of the expenses, attorney fees, her trustee fees, etc., off the top and then took her 20 percent share of what was left of the $40,000. She did this even though she knew her mother wanted her to pay the expenses of settling the trust and maintaining the house until it was transferred from her share of the $40,000. The brothers were angry with this. Effectively, she left them nothing but a few dollars.

Obviously, Jan was the wrong person to be the trustee. If one of the brothers or even a third party had been selected, there would most likely have been a better result—one that more accurately reflected Dorothy's wishes. Unfortunately, with Jan's interference, Dorothy's final communication with her sons was tainted.

In another case, Martha made the right choice. A widow, Martha also had three children, all boys. Martha lived close to her two youngest sons, but the oldest son lived across the country. A few months prior to her death, Martha visited Jeanne wanting to change certain provisions in her trust relating to her appointment of the successor trustee.

Originally, Martha had named her middle son as successor trustor because of his close proximity and because she perceived him as having the keenest business sense of the three. However, she had observed her middle son's behavior toward his younger brother during the past couple of years. She had come to the conclusion that he was going to be too bossy and controlling as a trustee to promote harmony in the family. Her youngest son was geographically closer than the oldest son, and he could have handled the trustee duties. Yet, Martha felt the "baby" of the family did not have the strength and experience that would be required to deal with the middle brother in a mature and adult way. Martha decided that the oldest son was the best for the job, even though he lived farthest away and was the only one of her sons who was not a degreed professional.

Time showed that Martha was absolutely right. After Martha's death, her oldest son worked with Jeanne to settle the estate. The middle brother immediately began to assert his right to take charge and expressed his surprise and anger that his mother had not named him as trustee. The older brother, in a mature and non-combative way, held his ground. He listened to the middle brother's advice in a respectful way and even assigned him some of the tasks that needed to be done.

The middle brother, for some reason, seemed to take his frustrations out on his younger brother, declaring that the youngest had bilked money out of their mother and now owed it back. In his anger, he also tried to persuade the trustee to deduct money from the younger brother's share. The older brother, as trustee, refused to give credence to these accusations, since there was nothing about their mother's trust or bank accounts that indicated any such activities had taken place. Eventually, the middle brother's accusations died down and were dropped. The trustee made sure everyone was informed of the true situation at all times and that they were each being treated equally and fairly.

The trust was settled, and the proceeds were split equally among the three brothers. They were all happy with the way everything was conducted, and they remain loving brothers and close friends today. They also have fond memories of their mother and are satisfied with the way she expressed her love to them in the transfer of her estate. Her careful evaluation as to which son would best handle the settlement of her trust paid off in terms of leaving her family emotionally intact.

What is the lesson to be learned from these two examples? Choosing a personal successor trustee requires thought and judgment. It is just as important to name a person who has the maturity and personality to generate a happy and loving result as it is to select a person with sound financial or business acumen. A trustor should never allow beneficiaries to influence this decision or to persuade him or her to select them as trustees. Even though a beneficiary may be the trustor's primary caretaker or may be a co-signer on a bank account, that person could be, and often is, the worst choice for trustee. Frequently, they are too emotionally involved and too close to the situation to see it clearly enough, and their own desires often seem to come ahead of what is best for everyone involved.

Choosing Your Successor Trustee

What are the attributes of a good successor trustee? Following are some of the most important characteristics to consider (we have listed these characteristics in what we feel is the order of importance):

First, the right trustee will be absolutely honest and, whether they agree with the distribution plan or not, will act completely in accordance with the letter and the spirit of what the trustor wants. Trustees have to make decisions. When putting a trust together, it is impossible to anticipate all circumstances that will apply and all the questions that may arise. A trustor, therefore, must instruct the trustee as to the feeling and attitude to be conveyed to the heirs. In other words, a trustee must understand the true message a trustor is trying to send and why certain decisions were made in setting up the trust. Choosing a trustee who can honestly carry out the trustor's wishes is even more important if a trustor has made any decisions that will not be easily accepted by one or more of the heirs. You can see how this would be especially true if a trustor has chosen to make an unequal distribution or to leave a loved one out of the trust completely.

Second, a trustee should be someone who is strong in character but who will not create controversy, seeking instead to prevent it as much as possible. The trustee should be someone who can make fair and nonjudgmental decisions that promote harmony and peace within the family. In the trust itself, the trustor should state his or her rationale behind selecting the trustee. Doing so will strengthen the trustee's position, creating greater cooperation among the heirs. It will also reinforce the trustor's message and desire for a fair and equitable resolution of the estate.

Third, a trustee must be willing to act in that position. No one should ever be coerced to take this job, nor should anyone be expected to do it based on his or her relationship to the trustor. A lot of work goes into managing even a simple trust, and a trustee must be willing to take on these duties. In addition, payment should be discussed and the trustor should include, within the language of the trust, explicit terms detailing the payment a trustee is to receive. Merely marshalling the assets, not to mention dealing with all the emotions and issues of the heirs, can be a daunting task for a trustee, but the trustor can make this job much easier by thoughtful preparation and planning.

Fourth, a trustee should be emotionally stable enough to handle the loss of the trustor along with the stress of dealing with all the legal issues. While it is true that many trusts, especially if they are well drafted by an experienced estate planning attorney, make the legal transfer less stressful because the majority of issues were well thought out when the trust was created, even simple estates can have unanticipated legal issues arise. These issues require solid judgment and emotional maturity from the trustee.

Fifth, a trustee should have average business judgment and be capable of thoroughly understanding the financial transactions that will have to take place after the trustor dies. In our experience, we have seen that business judgment is less important than the other traits we have listed. An expert in the financial area of concern can always be hired if a trustee needs assistance in these matters.

As you make decisions for your own trust, remember that your trustee is your main ally. This person will be your ambassador for your last communication with your heirs. Select your trustee with utmost care.

CHAPTER 12

FUNDING YOUR LIVING TRUST

When we speak about "funding," with respect to any trust, we mean putting assets into the trust by transferring the title of the asset from the owner (the trustor) to the trust. Just as with other trusts, the living trust can be unfunded, partially funded, or fully funded. Funding can occur during the lifetime of the trustor or after the trustor has died.

Unfunded Living Trusts

If no assets have been transferred to the trust, it is a meaningless document until such time as it is funded with some type of asset(s). Establishing a trust without transferring the title of the asset is the equivalent of opening a bank account without depositing any funds in the account. We don't know of a single bank that would agree to do this. In many states, however, a trust can be funded with only intangible assets, such as the ownership title to an insurance policy, which creates the expectation that at some future time money will be paid into the trust. Other states do not go along with this illusion, requiring instead that something of actual intrinsic value to be placed in the trust at the time of execution. Usually, a small sum of cash will suffice. In most states, it's possible to create a living trust, fund it with no more than $10, and then name the trust as the beneficiary of the trustor's life insurance policies, pension funds, and annuities. With such a trust, the funds from the insurance policies and annuities would go to one place when the trustor died. Then, there could either be a comprehensive distribution of those assets or sub-trusts could be set up. If a trustor's only assets are life insurance policies and pension funds, an unfunded living trust named as beneficiary of the policies and funds may make sense. Your estate planning attorney will be able to advise you on your state's guidelines.

If there are other assets, we can't really see any value in creating an unfunded revocable living trust, as this would put the other assets at risk for ending up in probate. This would also mean that assets would not be available to the trustor as needed if he/she should become disabled. Unless there is good reason to do otherwise, we are adamant that our clients put all of their assets into the trust. This act gives them the greatest access to the unique benefits of the living trust. Failure to fully fund the living trust is one of the common problems we see when inexperienced attorneys or untrained professionals prepare such documents.

Funded Living Trusts

How does funding a living trust work? As we mentioned previously, a trust is a written agreement between the trustor and the trustee. In that agreement, the trustor agrees to transfer certain property he or she owns to the trust.

Is this all that is required to fund the trust? No, this does not transfer any interest in the property to the trust without further action being taken to actually change the title of the asset to the name of the trust. So far it is only a promise to "fund" those properties to the trust at some time in the future. For example, John and Jane own a house, a bank account, and a stock account. They sign a trust agreement that says that they will transfer all of the property presently owned by them to the trust. Now they must do something more to actually keep their promise.

How then do they fund the trust with these properties? Each requires a different type of action. The house will require a deed to be drafted actually transferring all their right title and interest in the house to themselves as trustees of the trust. Usually that deed is then recorded with the county recorder's office where the property is located. The bank account is transferred by physically going to the bank and signing over the account again to John and Jane as trustees of the John and Jane Trust. The same action is required for the stock accounts. Once this is done, the trust now holds the legal title to these assets.

Does the trustee now get to live in the house or actually spend the money for himself? Yes, if he is the beneficiary of the trust. The right to possess the house and use the money belongs to the beneficiaries; all the trust owns is the "bare legal title to the assets." This is enough, however, to give the trustees legal authority to sign a deed to the house or sign checks on the trust bank accounts as well as manage the stock portfolio.

Remember that in most cases a revocable living trust initially has the same person for the trustor, trustee, and beneficiary. It's normally only upon the death of the trustor that a third party (the successor trustee) comes into the picture.

What is the practical effect of choosing to fully fund a living trust? As a trustor of such a trust, you would still own all of the property, just as you always did. The trustor gives up none of the control during his or her lifetime, but when the trustor dies, the property is automatically transferred to the person named as trustee. As we have explained, when a trustor dies, the trustee may access the trustor's bank accounts and stock accounts, as well as sign deeds or bills of sale to any properties the trustor has left behind without the necessity of going through the probate process. However, this is true only of the assets that have been funded to the trust. Those assets that remained in the trustor's name will need to be probated. A fully funded trust keeps the estate out of probate. Failure to fully fund a trust can cause problems for the heirs if the assets that are left out of the trust exceed the state threshold to probate. The following stories demonstrate the type of problems that may occur.

One of Jeanne's clients owned treasury bonds that he never transferred to his living trust because he thought it would cost too much in capital gains tax to do so. When he died, the value of the bonds greatly exceeded his state's threshold for probate. This meant, in addition to the trust settlement, a separate probate proceeding was required in order for the trustee to obtain title to these bonds. It wasn't until six months after the man died that the probate procedure even started. Probate will cost the estate a lot of money that could have been saved if the bonds had been transferred to the trust during the trustor's lifetime.

In another case, an elderly trustor, upon the advice of her financial planner, decided to place only her house and its contents in her trust. Because she wanted to leave these assets to her daughter, the woman named her daughter as the sole beneficiary. In addition to the house, the elderly woman owned some certificates of deposit. These she wanted to have divided equally between her two sons as their share of the estate. She didn't place these certificates in her trust. Instead, she named her sons as the direct beneficiaries of these funds.

Sometime later, a bank employee told her she needed to transfer the CD titles to her trust. Apparently, having forgotten why she had kept the CDs separate (or perhaps never really understanding in the first place) she transferred the certificates to the trust. Because the trust didn't name her sons as beneficiaries, she had unintentionally disinherited her sons altogether. Luckily, one of her sons happened to become aware of this situation and brought his mother to see Jeanne. Jeanne amended the trust to include the sons as beneficiaries. What could have been a very unfortunate situation was avoided, and all turned out well.

We believe that, <u>in most cases, all the assets owned by the trustor must be funded to the trust</u>. This keeps it simple. Some attorneys leave bank checking accounts out of the trust. We believe such exclusions must be considered on a case-by-case basis. Often, for convenience sake, a trustor will have a child as a joint signer on a small checking account so the child can assist the trustor in paying bills if that becomes necessary. This is sometimes not a bad idea, since such an arrangement can make paying the trustor's last expenses or other costs much easier. However, we recommend these accounts be limited in the amount of money they contain and that they are available for a specific purpose only. If a trustor needs more help than this on a continuing basis, it is probably better to appoint a co-trustee to serve with the trustor.

Other than a few exceptions (which we've noted), all other assets should be funded to the trust. In addition, all other distributions should be handled by the trustee to avoid unnecessary expense or unintended fiascoes. There are always exceptions to these guidelines, and your estate planning attorney can provide the best advice in this area as they relate to your specific needs.

In funding the trust, not all assets are treated the same. The manner and the time of funding vary, depending on the type of asset. Some assets, such as clothing and household goods, may be placed in the trust by a simple blanket assignment. With a blanket assignment, all items of a particular nature, such as household furnishings, even including any additional items of that nature that may be acquired later by the trustor, are transferred in total to the trust.

Other assets require a more formal assignment and notice to another party. Still others require that notice be given, such as in assignment of a lease. In addition, the transfer must be recorded and/or approved by the other party to the transaction. In some cases, certain assets are specifically left out of the trust in order to transfer them directly to a beneficiary outside the trust.

Ownership of insurance policies and annuities are not, as a rule, transferred to the revocable living trust. Instead, the trust is simply made the primary beneficiary. This allows the proceeds from these types of assets to flow into the trust and be distributed as part of the overall plan, which eliminates the possibility of unplanned changes in distribution among the beneficiaries.

On the other hand, IRAs, 401(k)'s and other types of pension plans must remain titled to the personal owner during his or her lifetime in order to avoid adverse tax consequences. If the plan's owner is married, the spouse will be named the primary beneficiary of these assets since spouses have rollover rights not available to third parties, including trusts. The trust will be named as the contingent (or secondary) beneficiary. In most cases, if the owner is not married, the trust will be the primary beneficiary. Then, upon distribution, the beneficiaries will pay income tax on the full amount of these funds since the trustor wasn't required to pay taxes on these funds during his or her lifetime. The taxes on these funds will be assessed at the beneficiaries' tax rate at the time of the distribution. For this reason, and because the tax laws are constantly changing, careful planning with an attorney and your accountant is called for in order to achieve the best tax treatment possible.

Funding a revocable living trust is a much easier process than funding other types of trusts because there are not as many decisions to make regarding the tax consequences of the funding. Except for those just mentioned, transfers of assets to a revocable living trust do not have any tax consequences to the trustor.

Since the transfer can be rescinded or revoked, the IRS doesn't require, nor will it allow, a separate tax return to be filed for a revocable living trust. All income to the trust remains personal to the trustors and is reported as part of the trustor's 1040 tax return. In all states, the transfer of real property to the trust is treated as only a change in formal title (not an actual change in ownership), which does not require a reassessment for property tax purposes.

While the transfer of assets to a living trust is easier tax wise, it can still be fraught with legal pitfalls for the uninformed. An example of such a pitfall would be in regard to joint tenancy property. While seemingly a simple concept, holding property in joint tenancy is a good example of how "simple" can be dangerous. The critical point to remember is the transfer of a joint tenancy interest to the trust effectively destroys the joint tenancy. While the legal reasons are too technical to go into here, suffice it to say that a trust cannot legally hold title as a joint tenant. As you may remember from our previous discussion, joint tenancy property has a special right of survivorship aspect. This means that, upon the death of one tenant, the surviving tenant automatically owns 100 percent of the property. A lack of understanding regarding how this relates to trusts can lead to disastrous results. Paul's story is the perfect example.

Paul's father died after a long and expensive illness that left his mother, Betty, with very little to live on except a few thousand dollars in her savings account and her Social Security benefits. Paul and his wife, Pam, wanted to help Betty buy a condo in which to live. Paul has two sisters and a brother, who isn't particularly friendly toward Paul. None of Paul's siblings were willing to contribute to Betty's financial welfare.

Title to the condo read: Paul and Pam, husband and wife, as joint tenants with Betty, a single woman. Paul and Pam were told that if the title was held this way, the house would revert to them automatically when Betty died, without the necessity of probate or even a will. They were also told that if something should happen to them, the condo would automatically belong to Betty.

Paul makes most of the payments on the property and claims all the tax benefits. This is fine until Betty gets a phone call from Sam, an annuity salesman. Sam introduces himself to Betty on the premise that he could assist her with her estate planning. Sam engages Betty in a conversation regarding a wondrous new thing called a "living trust." Betty tells Sam that she doesn't own anything but the condo, which she owns with her son, and a small savings account, which is in trust for her children equally. Sam informs Betty that if she doesn't put these assets in a living trust, when she dies her children will have to go through a terrible process called probate, which will cost them thousands of dollars and a lot of time and stress.

This is not true, but Betty doesn't know that (Sam probably doesn't know that either), so she agrees to let Sam come over and explain it. Sam arrives at the appointed time. He is charming and seems concerned for Betty's well-being. He sympathizes with the loss of her husband and even offers to help Betty fix a leaky faucet that Paul hasn't had time to work on. Finally, they get down to business, and Sam convinces Betty that he has to find out all about her finances so he can determine what she needs to do to get her affairs in order. He discovers that not only does she have her interest in the condo, but she also has more in her savings account than she had indicated at first. Sam convinces Betty to buy a living trust. Sam has no clue about the meaning of joint tenancy ownership. Sam is simply doing what he was trained to do—sell a trust. Sam tells Betty the trust will only cost a few hundred dollars and will save her children thousands.

Betty resists, telling Sam that she should talk to her children first, but Sam is a good salesman. He convinces Betty that she is doing her children a great favor and says she can even name one of them as the trustee of the trust. Betty wants to be fair to all of her children, so Sam suggests she name them to succeed her in the order of their ages, beginning with the oldest. He tells her that her children don't need to be involved until after she dies, but that she can leave everything to them equally. He mistakenly assures Betty that by putting her half of the condo in the living trust, nothing will change that will affect Paul's half ownership. Betty knows her children are busy people, and she doesn't want to be a bother. Besides, Sam tells Betty that if something were to incapacitate her, the children could just step right in and manage all of her affairs much more easily if everything was in the trust. So, while she doesn't really understand all the ramifications, Betty is convinced and writes Sam a check for preparation of the trust. Betty still thinks Paul will inherit her half of the condo when she dies.

Sam prepares Betty's trust by making slight changes to a trust prepared by some law firm years earlier. Sam also prepares a quit-claim deed to the condo, naming Betty's trust as joint owner of half of the property. Sam does have an attorney he consults with from time to time, but he can't see any reason to talk with an attorney regarding this "simple" case.

Several days later, Sam calls Betty to tell her that her trust is ready to be signed. He takes it to her home, she signs, and he notarizes all of the documents. At that time, Sam tells Betty that she should really put most of her money into an annuity. He convinces her that this would protect her family if she were in need of long-term nursing care. Having cared for her late husband when he was sick, Betty agrees that she would like to save her children the struggles of having to provide for her care. Betty gives Sam most of her savings to put into the annuity. Besides, she thinks Sam is a nice young man who is acting only in her best interest. In fact, Sam may even believe he is acting in Betty's best interest when, in reality, just the opposite was true.

A few weeks later, having said nothing to the children about the trust, Betty dies very unexpectedly. The trust document which names Paul's older brother as the successor trustee, and divides all of the assets of the trust equally between Paul and his siblings, is discovered. Paul's brother consults an estate planning attorney to guide him in settling the trust's affairs. The attorney reviews the title to the property and the terms of the annuity. To avoid a large penalty for early withdrawal, the money in the annuity must be distributed on a five-year monthly payout of principal and interest to the children. This penalty will apply over the next 15 years on a decreasing percentage scale. At the present time, the penalty is at 15 percent. This is not good news. There are not enough liquid funds in the estate to cover the bills. The annuity will have to be cashed in. The attorney tells the trustee (Paul's older brother) that the condo is titled half to Paul and half to the trust. Since the trust cannot legally hold title as a joint tenant, the trust holds the title as a tenant in common by default. This means there is no right of survivorship. Under the terms of the trust, the trust's share belongs equally to the four children.

Paul is livid. He paid for this condo, yet his brother is adamant that the condo is trust property. Paul wonders how in the world his mother could have done this to him. Paul consults an attorney, seeking to have the transfer of the property to the trust nullified. Ultimately, he wins the lawsuit based on the legal insufficiency of the trust documents themselves and on substantial evidence that joint tenancy was the real intent of the parties. Because Paul won, his and his brother's attorney fees are paid by the trust, which means that thousands of dollars are deducted from the diminished amount left from the sale of the annuity.

How do the children feel about Mom's last communication? They can't really be angry with her, can they? She really wasn't at fault, was she?

Paul, at least, and possibly the others, may have felt some resentment that their mother hadn't consulted them before she made such a major decision. Betty's last impression wasn't what she intended it to be. It certainly didn't promote unity and closeness between her children. Now Paul and his older brother really have issues, and the other children are not happy with the outcome either.

Moral to the story: Whenever legal transfer of any property is contemplated, an informed opinion by a trained legal professional is required. <u>Legal transfers are seldom as simple as they appear, and the ramifications can be costly in many ways.</u>

As more and more people are using revocable living trusts as their primary estate planning vehicle, the funding of assets to such trusts is being accepted as standard procedure by the institutions typically involved (such as banks, title companies, stock brokerages, and insurance companies). The drawbacks encountered just a few years ago are now being eliminated, and delaying the funding of such trusts is becoming less and less attractive.

Just a short time ago, holding title to property in a revocable living trust was unique and unheard of in many places. Some states required the entire trust be recorded in order to hold title to real property in the name of the trust. Similarly, when the property was sold, title companies also required a full copy of the trust. Most brokerage houses, title companies, and banks also demanded a full copy. These requirements negated the privacy benefits of the trust because all of the aspects of the trust were disclosed to numerous persons. Today, these requirements have been eliminated in most areas. Presently, almost without exception, a deed from the trustor to the trust is acceptable for recording. Banks and brokerage houses readily accept a brief abstract of certain parts of the trust along with a certificate, signed and notarized by the trustors, verifying the trust's existence and authority. Banks usually do not require that a checking account transferred to the trust even be designated as a trust account, nor do they require that the trustee sign checks as a trustee. This has largely eliminated the objection most people had to funding checking accounts to a trust.

It is clear that the use of the revocable living trust sets the modern trend for estate planning and is rapidly becoming the most widely recognized, acceptable, and honored way of titling much of the property owned by individuals in this country. As a result of this trend, there are few reasons for failure to fund these trusts during the lifetime of the trustors. The major exception would be those items that must remain titled personally to the trustors, such as IRAs and pension plans.

Taking Title

How should property within the trust be titled? Title should not be transferred to the trust in general, such as to the "Jones Family Trust." Someone capable of signing a signature should hold title. So, rather than in the name of the trust, the title is usually and preferably held in the name of the trustee(s). For example, to transfer title to any property to the Jones Family Trust, we would transfer it to "Ed Jones and Edith Jones, as trustees of the Jones Family Trust, initially created on the 10th day of March, 2000." Often this type of title will be abbreviated. In this case, the title would read: "Ed Jones and Edith Jones, UTD, 3/10/2000." The UTD stands for "Under Trust Dated" and is perfectly acceptable.

To transfer something in the future, such as a beneficiary designation on an insurance policy, we prefer the beneficiary designation to be stated in this way: "Then Acting Trustee of the Jones Family Trust, initially created on the 10th day of March, 2000".

In conclusion:

1. Revocable living trusts are not sensitive to tax issues when funded.

2. Funding a revocable living trust appears to be simple but can cause undesirable results if done without expert knowledge and planning.

3. The funding of living trusts is accepted by most institutions today. If titled properly, few problems are encountered when later removing the assets from such trusts.

4. It is best to fund the trust with all the assets during the trustor's lifetime, unless there are significant and well-understood reasons to leave some assets out of the trust.

5. It is generally simpler and more desirable to name the trust as beneficiary of all insurance policies and annuities, when there is no spouse, and as contingent beneficiary of all IRA or other tax deferred assets when there is a living spouse.

6. Checking accounts should be titled to the trust, unless there is a compelling reason to have a small account held in the name of another person for a specific, limited purpose.

7. Title to trust assets should always be transferred to the trustees of the trust.

CHAPTER 13

LOVING LANGUAGE IS WORTH ITS WEIGHT IN GOLD

The revocable living trust is the most flexible and, for most estates, the most useful tool for creating the beginnings of an estate plan that will leave a loving last impression. In fact, for many people, the revocable living trust is the only tool they will need. Some people, particularly those with larger estates or complicated issues, will need to use other tools in addition to the revocable living trust to effectively protect their estate against estate taxes. Your estate planning attorney will help you determine which tools are most appropriate for your particular situation.

The examples in this book are intended to illustrate some of the emotional and financial hazards that can occur when people fail to properly plan ahead for what will happen with their estate when they die. The results are often tragic and long lasting. The final communication from an estate owner can have a significant and powerful impact on those left behind. In this chapter, we want to show you ways to make that last communication extremely positive by using loving language, both in verbal and written form.

Through most of this book we have written to a general audience, knowing that estate planners, potential heirs, and professionals in the estate planning arena will all be reading this book. However, since this chapter focuses on the most personal aspects of the estate plan, we will assume that you, the reader, are an estate owner and we will speak directly to these matters.

STARTING ON A PLAN

Having taken the first step of deciding to create an estate plan, the next thing for you to do is to prepare a written inventory. By this, we do not mean a listing of personal property, such as clothing, jewelry, and family china and silver. Rather, create a list of your real property, bank accounts, stock accounts, IRAs, and other pension plans. In addition, list any business interests and automobiles, as well as the estimated value of household furnishings, jewelry of major value ($5,000 and up), and any other collections or items of substantial value. (See the forms provided for this inventory in Chapter Three.) This is another situation where the use of estate planning software may be extremely valuable.

Now, think about which individuals you would like to receive your property when you die. Make sure you think about the small items of personal property that we mentioned in the previous paragraph, and consider which of these items you want to leave to specific people. This is also a good time for you to decide whether a charity is to receive part of your estate.

The next step will greatly assist you in leaving the final communication you desire. While we consider this step to be vitally important, it is often overlooked, particularly by estate planning professionals who focus only on the mechanics and the legalities of the estate transfer. To begin, we recommend you think about the people you have chosen as heirs to your estate. Then, write some notes about your personal relationships and your memories of these people. If you have chosen to leave out a seemingly obvious heir, such as one of your children, explain in writing your reasons for disinheriting him or her. Similarly, if you have chosen to make an unequal distribution, explain your reasons. As you write, contemplate your decisions carefully and imagine yourself in the place of the child who is to receive less. <u>Consider how each of your heirs will feel when they learn of your decisions and think about what you can do to produce the most loving result possible.</u>

As we have noted previously, the relative wealth of your children should never be the basis for an unequal distribution among your heirs. <u>Never assume that the child who is receiving less will feel fine about this simply because he or she doesn't need the money</u>. Such assumptions are perhaps the surest way to cause major problems in the family.

Once you have made these decisions and explained your reasons in writing, take time to choose the best person to act as your successor trustee and effectively settle your estate. Again, as you think about your selection, keep in mind that your goal is to pass your estate without creating family havoc. Consider the attributes we suggested in the chapter on choosing your trustee.

Once you have made these decisions, it may be appropriate to call a family meeting to discuss your plans. You may also want your estate planning attorney to attend and help explain the details. While in some families this may create undue dissension, we have found a meeting can help in most cases. At the meeting, explain how the assets are to be distributed and why. Tell your heirs whom you have chosen to act as trustee, and explain why you have made that decision as well. Ask your heirs to honestly express their opinions, particularly if they differ from yours. Be willing to listen closely to what they say. Remember that their comments may very well be understated because they do not want to offend you. At the same time, they may have some good alternative solutions that should be considered.

If a family meeting is not possible because of distance or other reasons, you may want to call each person separately and inform them of your decisions. If conflict or concerns arise, work until all is resolved. If conflicts can't be resolved or matters can't be agreed upon, bring your estate planning attorney into the picture and let him or her assist you. Your attorney may have some suggestions or alternatives that will help satisfy the other parties' concerns while allowing you to meet your goals. An attorney can often help facilitate communication without taking sides or becoming overly emotional.

If, for some reason, you cannot, or simply don't want to, involve your heirs in this process, take the time necessary to think about the ramifications of your plan on each of your children. Then insist on having language in the trust portfolio that will enlighten each child as to the reasons for your decisions. If your planning is done in the spirit of love and respect for each person involved, and that spirit is then expressed in writing, the results should be very positive. We don't recommend doing the planning without the involvement of your heirs unless it is absolutely prohibitive to involve them. We believe it is far better to do the planning together, because when the time comes that the plan is put in motion, you will no longer be around to rectify any problems that may present themselves. Remember, it may take courage and real honesty to meet face to face, but doing so gives you a much better opportunity to accomplish the results you want.

DISCOVER YOUR TRUE SITUATION

After you have decided on what you will do with your estate, there are three possibilities for implementing your plan. First, you may decide that you are not going to create a formal estate plan. Second, you may choose to have your attorney prepare either a will or a revocable living trust, which has a personal trustee. Third, you may decide to have an attorney prepare a revocable living trust, which has a corporate trustee or a combination of a personal and a corporate trustee. How do you decide?

In every case, you should consult with an estate planning attorney to discuss the alternatives you should consider based on the assets in your estate. This consultation will not cost a lot and is worth every penny. Often, an attorney will give a consultation free or at a reduced fee. If you have prepared as we have suggested above, or with the help of a template, the consultation will be shorter and, thus, less expensive. This consultation is a must. You cannot evaluate your estate planning situation without professional guidance. Work with an attorney, and follow your attorney's suggestions. If you disagree with your attorney, seek the consultation of a second estate planning attorney and compare their advice. The small added expense is worth your peace of mind.

WORKING WITH YOUR ATTORNEY

How do you go about finding the right attorney? Remember that it is important this person be qualified to advise you in the area of estate planning, so be careful to explore his or her background. We don't say this to discredit the abilities of any attorney but simply to emphasize that estate planning is a very complicated and specialized area. The attorney you choose should be one who devotes the majority of his or her practice to this type of work.

While working with an attorney, you will most likely need to take control of certain aspects of your planning in order to accomplish the kind of communication you want. You can focus on the messages that are important to send and leave the legal aspects of the plan to your attorney. When interviewing your attorney, explain that you want to include personal, loving messages in your trust. Be prepared to tell your attorney how you want these messages worded. Assure your attorney that you are not going to try to suggest wording for any areas that would change the legal aspects in any way. Explain that you fully expect to discuss all legal ramifications of any changes that you are proposing. Also, because it will take a little more time and thought for both you and your attorney to personalize the wording, make it clear that you are willing to pay for the extra time. This minimal expense is well worth the effort it takes to create your perfect last impression. If the attorney balks at this or is negative about it, you might suggest that he or she get a copy of this book and read it. If that doesn't work, perhaps you have not yet found the right attorney—keep looking.

Loving and explanatory language in both the distribution of the trust and in the trustee appointment section is advisable. If you choose a corporate trustee, specific language may be required in your trust; you may need to accommodate the wishes of the corporate trustee regarding this wording. In that case, rather than changing the language of the trust itself, it may be necessary to use one or more of the alternatives listed below.

USE LOVING LANGUAGE

In most wills or trusts, the standard language presently used to leave property to one's children in equal shares goes something like this:

The trustee shall divide the trust estate into three equal shares and allocate one such equal share to each of the then living children of the trustors, or to the then living issue of a deceased child of the trustors in equal shares.

Obviously, this distribution assumes that the trustors have three children, each of whom is to receive one third of the estate. The language is clear, but it really doesn't invoke warm and fuzzy feelings, does it?

In the distribution language, listing the children or perhaps even the grandchildren, by name, would make it a little more friendly, but not much. Yet, notice how the feel of the message changes if we say something like this:

The trustee shall allocate one third (1/3) of the trust estate to our daughter, Susan, who we have adored since the day she was born and whose accomplishments in the world of art continually astonish and delight us; one third (1/3) to our son, Jim, our special friend, a business wizard and an outstanding husband and father; and one third (1/3) to our son, Bill, always the family sports fan, a great doctor and a greater golfer. What we couldn't spend, we lovingly leave for all of you to enjoy in any way you wish. Have fun. Always love each other. Our real treasures are the three of you. We leave these gifts as a token of our love, from your mom and dad.

Don't you think that sounds better? We do. If you were one of those three children, wouldn't this language of love make you feel adored and cherished by Mom and Dad? How would such a message make you feel toward your brothers and sisters? You can make your own trust language equally as loving, or even more so, by adding wording that makes your trust personal for you and your children.

What about other situations? For example, what words could be used if one of your children had died and his or her share of the trust was to go to the grandchildren? Obviously, if the grandchildren were already living, we would most likely name them and tell them how much we love them, just as we did the children. What if there are only prospective grandchildren? Being called "then living issue" is not very endearing, is it? What about something like the following?

In the heartbreaking event that we should outlive one or more of you, then the trustee shall allocate your respective share to your children, whom we will love with all of our hearts just as we did you, so that they may share equally in what would have been yours to give them.

That language communicates love and caring, don't you think? How do you suppose the rest of the family would feel about that communication?

Jeanne occasionally has clients who want to create a trust with uneven distribution. At times, parents have already given or loaned money to a child or one of the children may have alienated him/herself from the family. How can such situations be handled in a loving way that will lessen any anguish or resentment that might be created? This question could also apply to situations in which there are no children but a lot of brothers and sisters or nieces and nephews who are not going to share equally, or at all, in the estate proceeds. We believe there should always be an explanation in these cases.

For instance, let's say there's a family with two daughters—one who has basically ignored her mother and the other who has always been there to help. The daughters are both in similar financial situations. Wording in the trust could read as follows:

The trustee shall distribute to my daughter, Susie Jones—the most adorable child anyone could ever want, smart as a whip, light of my life, great mother and wife, constant helpmate and confidante in my last years since her father died—my home and all belongings within it and one-half of the remainder of my estate. Thank you, Susie, for your extra thoughtfulness and kindness in these last years. I love you, Mom.

The trustee shall distribute the other half of the remainder of my estate to my other daughter, Ellen Smith. You are such an accomplished businesswoman, beautiful in every way. I am so proud of you. I love you, Mom.

Does including such wording take some of the sting out? We think so. <u>If an estate is to be unevenly distributed, a loving explanation is better than saying nothing at all</u>. Even though a parent may be angry or disappointed with a child, the child is most likely still loved, and the parent can express that love in a final communication. In fact, because a parent's final communication is so important to children, such a communication could mend hurt feelings and could even help to support a child in making necessary changes in his or her life.

CARL'S CASE REVISITED

Remember Carl? He was the child who was left entirely out of his mother's distribution. Even though Carl had suggested that she leave everything to his sister, he was devastated when his mother did exactly that. As a result, Carl and his sister, who had always been close, became estranged. What could Carl's mother have done differently so he would have had a much more loving reaction to the distribution she made?

What if the trust had read as follows?

The trustee is to distribute the sum of $10,000 to my son, Carl, whom I love with all of my heart. Carl, I am so proud of all of your accomplishments, and I am impressed and honored by your selfless generosity in suggesting that your sister receive the bulk of my estate, since you are in a good financial position and she is not. You bring such joy and laughter to all who know you. You have always been the light of my life, even though you never became that great violinist that I wanted you to be. (Ha! Ha!) I love you, Carl, Mom.

The trustee shall distribute the remaining balance of my estate to my beloved daughter, Helen, who has given up so much of her own life to take care of me in these last years of my life. Helen, you have had such a financial struggle to single-handedly raise your three beautiful children, and you have done a wonderful job. Thank you for putting up with me so faithfully all of these years. I know it has not been easy. I love you, Helen, Mom.

Do you think Carl may have reacted differently and that he and his sister may have been able to remain close if this language had been used? We can't say for sure, but we think such language could have made a big difference.

LEAVING A CHILD OUT ALTOGETHER:

It is not uncommon for parents to choose to leave one or more of their children out of the will or trust entirely. Often, there is good reason for this seemingly drastic act of disinheriting one of the children. Whatever the reasons may be, the parents' decision should always be explained in the trust, and each of the children, particularly the one being disinherited, should be addressed in loving, supportive language. If a child is left out and no explanation is given, a devastating lasting impression could be the result.

The traditional wording used to exclude a child goes something like this:

I (we) have intentionally and specifically failed to provide for our son, John Smith, under the terms of this trust agreement.

How is that for cold language? We believe there are some ways to soften that message and express a great deal more love and caring.

So, what if the son, named John Smith, is to be left out of the will or trust because he has already received his share of his parents' property? Maybe the parents could use the following language to ease the situation in this case:

We have intentionally failed to provide for our beloved son, John, under the terms of this trust agreement. During our lives, we were glad to furnish him money to build his new home. This represents our gift to him, which would have otherwise come to him as part of this trust. John and his wife, Karen, and their two children, Frankie and Alan, are so very dear to us. John, you have always been there when we needed you. You were the most beautiful little boy we have ever seen and just as smart as a whip. John, you will always be a success in life no matter what you do. We love you with all our hearts. Love, Mom and Dad.

Better? We think so.

Sometimes, parents are unsure of how to handle a situation in which a child has demonstrated an inability to handle money responsibly. Perhaps a child has been in trouble with the law, has an alcohol or drug addiction or is simply irresponsible and untrustworthy. Rather than completely disinheriting a child, these situations can be handled with ongoing trust provisions. For example, a trust could include provisions that would allow the child to receive a portion of the inheritance only if certain conditions were met (i.e., in the case of drug or alcohol problems, a child may be required to complete a recovery program, etc.)

In some cases in dealing with a child who has such a problem, parents may feel that attaching conditions may not work or is not an acceptable solution. Still, if a parent chooses to leave a child out of the will or trust, the child can be addressed with love and respect in the trust document.

Remember how cold the traditional language sounds:

I (we) have intentionally and specifically failed to provide for our son, Jaime, under the terms of this trust agreement.

Perhaps the following language could be used:

I (we) have intentionally and specifically failed to provide for my son, Jamie, in this trust instrument. Jamie is presently suffering from an addiction to drugs and has been so afflicted for many years. I have lost hope that Jamie will recover from this addiction. Therefore, even though I love him with all of my heart and devoutly pray for his full recovery, I do not choose to leave him any means to pursue his affliction in the future.

These situations can be tough. It can be heartbreaking for parents to think there is no hope for their child. Unfortunately, there are times when tough calls need to be made and problems need to be addressed head on. However, remember, if something miraculous happens and a child gets into recovery or otherwise has a turn around during the parents' lifetime, the trust can always be amended to include that child.

Another situation, which is common in America today, is when children from a prior marriage are involved. We strongly suggest a trust be set up in order to keep the children of one of the spouses, usually the one who passes away first, from being disinherited. If you are in a second, or subsequent, marriage, with children from any prior marriages, we strongly recommend you consult an estate planning attorney. Otherwise, there is a good chance that your last impression will be very poor.

Let's consider an example of a couple in a second marriage with a small estate, which is under the federal $2,000,000 inheritance tax credit amount. The couple decides to split the property down the middle and give half of the community property to the husband's children and half to the wife's, without making any adjustment based on how many children each person has. Typical language in a trust designed to handle this type of situation goes like this:

Upon the death of the last trustor to die, the trustee shall divide the trust into two equal portions, one said portion shall be distributed in equal shares to the then living children of the Husband trustor, and one said portion shall be distributed in equal shares to the then living children of the Wife trustor, all distributions to be free and clear of the trust.

This is not an example of loving language, nor is the arrangement the best. A better way to plan in this situation would be to have separate trusts, or at a minimum, to split the trust at the time the first spouse dies. This would give the couple much more flexibility and leave less confusion among the heirs. It also allows each parent to provide for his/her own children in his/her own way. However, at the very least, if the couple decides not to have separate trusts, the following language could help:

The trustee shall divide the trust into two equal shares of 50 percent. It is our desire to distribute our estate equally between our children. Each of us has committed everything we had to our marriage, and since then we have acquired everything together. Regardless of whichever one of us passes first, we want our spouse to live as comfortably as possible and with full use of all the assets of our life together. If there are assets remaining after the survivor of us passes, we want those assets to be shared equally between our respective children.

Therefore, the trustee shall distribute one such 50-percent share equally between Fred's three children: Alice, who puts the sparkle in our lives and is so much fun with her quirky sense of humor; June, a terrific mother and loving friend who has provided us with our precious grandchildren, Anthony and Tricia; and Billy, the fearless sky jumper and risk-taker who has made us so proud with his entrepreneurial spirit. We want each of you to know that we both love you with all our hearts.

The trustee shall distribute the remaining 50 percent share to Janet's daughter, Wendy, who is the light of her mother's life and who gives us both immeasurable joy and pleasure in our old age with her sweet and loving attitude. We both love you so much, Wendy.

Because this expression is clearer and more loving, it will do much more to fulfill the emotional needs of all concerned. The message is intended to spell out the trustors' distribution plan, clearly and specifically. The wording doesn't leave a lot of room for misunderstanding yet still communicates the important message of love.

Of course, there are innumerable situations, and we can't give examples of them all, or even of those that are the most common. However, from the few examples we have given, we hope you have been inspired to write the kind of language in your trust or your will that comes from your heart and touches the hearts of your heirs and beneficiaries.

LANGUAGE CONCERNING THE SELECTION OF TRUSTEES

Parents often express concern about choosing one of the children as the trustee to take over for them. They worry that those not chosen will be offended or will feel left out. If there are only two children, it may be proper to name them as co-trustees, particularly if they get along well. Having any more than two co-trustees becomes unmanageable and makes decision making complicated. We advise that not more than two trustees serve at one time. Sometimes trustors will choose the eldest child to serve, and then they list the others as backup trustees, in order of their birth. This is not a good way to decide on a trustee, as we explained in the section on choosing a trustee. In cases where the heirs may disagree with the choice of trustees, diplomatic language explaining why and how the choice was made may help eliminate possible conflict and hard feelings.

The usual trust language for the appointment of the trustees is cold, barren and without explanation. Here is an example:

The original trustee of the trust shall be George Smith. Upon his relinquishment of the duties of the trustee, the trustor appoints the following persons to serve as trustee in the order named:
Ted Smith
Cheryl Smith

The problem with using this standard language is that it neither reflects the father's real wishes nor does it communicate his love for his children. Let's look at what might be a better way to communicate.

In this case, there are four children. The father, George, thinks his son Ted would be able to promote harmony and goodwill among all of his heirs, so George believes that Ted would be the best choice to be his trustee. Ted is neither the smartest nor the most successful. He also lives the farthest distance away. Yet, he is the most levelheaded and is emotionally strong enough to do what needs to be done. Judith, the eldest child, lives near George and has been the closest to him. George believes that Judith will greatly resent his decision to name her brother as successor trustee. However, George realizes that Judith is too controlling and abrasive to handle the job without causing all kinds of havoc and hard feelings among the other children. How can he make this appointment in a way that will soften the blow to Judith's ego? Obviously, the usual language would be of little help.

What if the appointment were made in the following language:

The initial trustee of the trust shall be George Smith. Upon his relinquishment of the duties of the trustee, he appoints the following persons to act as trustee, in the order named.

I, George Smith, appoint my son, Ted Smith, to act as trustee upon my relinquishment of such duties. I have given a great deal of thought and consideration in making this appointment. It is my wish and my goal that all my children remain loving and respected friends with one another when I am gone. I believe that the settlement of my estate will either promote or hinder this result, and I believe that the person I choose to handle this matter will have a great impact in this respect. I did not make the choice based on any feelings of favoritism among my children. I made my choice in the belief that Ted's even, strong and temperate disposition makes him the best choice for the job. It was a tough decision, since each of you is well qualified in every way to serve in this capacity. Please help Ted as much as you can to accomplish my goals.

By drawing names out of a hat, I have chosen Cheryl as the backup trustee. Therefore, I, George Smith, appoint my gracious daughter, Cheryl Smith, to act as trustee in the event that her brother, Ted Smith, is not able or decides to decline the duties of the trustee.

Is it likely that Judith will react in a less resentful way to this language than she may have to the language that is traditionally used? We think so. George has made it perfectly clear why he chose Ted to be the trustee. His reasons were soundly based, and the rest of the family members most likely see the same qualities in Ted's personality that their father does. In George's explanation, none of the other children were made to feel put down or unloved by his choice. There was no inference that George in any way considered them to be less lovable or less intelligent than their brother. Would this same kind of language work in your case?

As you can no doubt imagine, your attorney isn't going to come up with this kind of language without your input. You will have to suggest to the attorney the wording you want to use in the trust provisions. There is no way he or she can do this without your help, since your attorney doesn't have a clue about your relationship to your children.

If you object to exposing these feelings or thoughts to an attorney, or if you feel uncomfortable with the idea that people outside of your immediate family may see these things if they are made a part of the trust, there are alternatives that can be considered. One such alternative is to include a "treasure letter" within the trust. We prefer the idea of including at least some personal language in the trust itself, because your words will more likely be preserved and read if they are an integral part of this document. However, a treasure letter is an acceptable alternative.

TREASURE LETTERS—AN ALTERNATIVE TO LOVING LANGUAGE IN THE TRUST

If, for some reason, you feel it is undesirable or inconvenient to include loving language within a trust document, a letter to each of your heirs that will promote your goal can be included in the trust portfolio. Each letter can be sealed and can remain confidential between you and the particular heir you are addressing. We feel, however, that it is beneficial for all of the children in a family to hear their parents' loving expressions to the other children, as well as to themselves. Sharing these messages seems to promote family unity, as your children are assured that they are all being treated openly with equal love and respect.

Interestingly, it has been our observation that in cases of unequal distributions, those who receive a larger part of the estate are often as negatively affected as those who do not receive a portion. There seems to be some guilt and shame attached to being the chosen one when another sibling receives less. This inequality often affects the relationship between the siblings, usually in a negative way. <u>When making decisions about handling your particular situation, remember any inequality may affect the relationships between your heirs</u>. Even when the children are treated equally in a will or trust, we feel a personal message to each child is greatly beneficial in promoting love, good feelings, and family unity. It seems as if these personal messages are best received and more beneficial to all concerned if they are written as part of an open letter to the entire family, rather than separate sealed and confidential messages. The choice, of course, is always up to you.

Based on our years of experience, we have found the best combination seems to be personalized, loving language within the trust document along with an open letter to the family with paragraphs written specifically for each child. Again, if you choose not to tailor the trust language to fit your situation, we strongly recommend that you consider at least writing an open, loving letter.

One more important note: When using letters to communicate with your heirs, it is important that your successor trustee be made aware of the existence of these letters and their whereabouts. Otherwise, the letters may never be discovered and read. Our suggestion is that the letters be placed in the trust portfolio with the trust document itself and that they be marked: IMPORTANT—OPEN UPON OUR DEATH.

LOVING LANGUAGE FOR SPOUSES

A loving last message for a spouse is an important issue that we have yet to address. Remember the man who lost his wife very unexpectedly in the middle of the night? They were fairly young, and they had no idea that such a thing could happen to them. We think every spouse should create a letter to his or her partner that could be read under such circumstances. We believe the grieving process could be greatly eased if such a letter existed. Such a letter might say, among other things:

No matter how we last parted, I love you more than anything in the world, and there is nothing I could not forgive. You are my true treasure, and I would not ever willingly part from you.

We believe such a letter may have helped the husband in the example we shared earlier. Don't you think it would have been easier, if he had such a letter, for him to forgive himself for the fight he and his wife had the night she died? We do.

COMMUNICATING WITHOUT A PLAN

Obviously, we do not recommend taking a "do nothing" approach when it comes to estate planning. (Review the chapter on the Do Nothing Plan.) We highly recommend one of the alternatives we have suggested in this book. However, even if you choose to do nothing else about planning to transfer your estate, at least consider leaving some message to those you love. Unfortunately, none of us has a crystal ball to tell us when it's time for us to leave this existence. Think about how you would want your family to remember you if you were to suddenly die tomorrow. What would they want to hear from you, and if the tables were turned, what would you want to hear from them?

Cathy's mother took her own life when Cathy was just a small child. Her mother left no message, and Cathy's father refused to discuss her mother's death. In fact, she and her father never became very close or learned how to communicate well with each other. All her life, Cathy has wondered why her mother did what she did. Was it Cathy's fault? Didn't her mother love her? This lack of communication has had a profound effect on Cathy's life. Then, when Cathy was in her 20s, her father died unexpectedly. Everyone was shocked. He had no estate plan, and he left no other form of communication. Everything he owned went to his second wife and then to her children. Cathy and her four brothers got nothing.

Cathy says, "I will always wonder why he didn't care enough to take care of my brothers and me. If only he had left me some word of love or some caring expression, I could have healed my resentments a lot faster and better. I feel just as bad for my brothers as I do for myself."

<u>The bottom line is communication!</u> With or without a formal plan, you can still leave an expression of your feelings for your family and loved ones. Write a letter to each of them, and tell them how precious they are to you. Do it today! Don't put it off. Write letters to your children, your close family members, and to other relatives and friends you care about as well. These

letters can form part of your estate plan later on, so writing them will not be time wasted should you decide to have a trust prepared in the future. Whether you set up a trust or not, by writing these letters, you will have at least put in place some message to those you will leave behind. This is an important step toward leaving the perfect last impression with those people you care about the most.

CHAPTER 14

DO'S AND DON'TS

This book has been designed to help eliminate many of the complications that can be associated with estate planning. More importantly, this book hopes to change the focus when it comes to estate planning by introducing the idea of estate planning as one of the most important forms of communicating with your heirs.

To reinforce some of the most important ideas, we have prepared a simple list of things to do and not to do. Use this section as a way to review and crystallize your ideas about estate planning and also as a checklist to help you get started with your own plan.

The "DO" List

1) DO plan your estate now.
Your last impression is inevitable. Sooner or later you will have to face it, so why not do so with as much composure and dignity as possible. There is little benefit in waiting until some future time to take action. If you begin your plan now but learn more or discover a better way in the future, you can always build on what you have started. People in great pain who are terminally ill or near death may not be thinking as clearly about their estate plan as they would have earlier. <u>If you do nothing</u>

now, you may lose the chance to plan as you would like. There is no better time than the present to begin.

2) DO survey and list all your assets.
Many of our clients have been surprised at the extent of their estate when they have undertaken the task of surveying and listing all their assets. Most of them, including those who previously thought they had nothing to leave anyone, decided that creating such a list was worth the effort. If nothing else, this activity provides a realistic picture of where a person stands economically and offers a chance to move forward with goals for the future. We have included a form in this book that can assist you in conducting a survey of your assets. While this form includes the items that most commonly make up an estate, do not consider this form to be a comprehensive list. You can also use the aid of an estate planning software program to assist you in preparing your list of assets. Include absolutely everything in your survey. Estimate each asset's current value as reasonably as you can without spending a great deal of money to acquire the estimates. You can often use the services of real estate brokers, for instance, to give you a fair market value of your real property. Dealers of all kinds are usually willing to help you value your cars, boat, collectibles, and memorabilia. Don't assume something has no value just because you have had it forever. If you have never done this before, you could be pleasantly surprised. Find out exactly where you stand economically.

3) DO decide who will receive items of personal property.
Make a list, either by the person's name or by the item to be received, to whom each item is to go. Store this list in a safe place,

and review it at least every three years. Share the list with your heirs and with your estate planning attorney. Modify it based on suggestions you receive from both. For example, if your daughter really wants the lovely pearl necklace you bought on your trip to Hong Kong and no one else is as eager to have it, you will have made a step in the right direction by giving her the piece. Don't be embarrassed about doing this. It is better for you to decide who gets what than for your heirs or your trustee to have to play the "gimme game" after you have passed away. By taking the time to inventory and assign each item, you will most likely be preventing the conflict that otherwise could arise between your heirs.

4) DO choose a professional estate planning attorney.
Estate planning is complicated and is a minefield for the uninitiated, so choose an attorney who specializes in this area of the law. Look for a person who is not only experienced but who is also open, friendly, and understanding of your needs. You should also look for someone with whom you feel a good rapport. Your attorney should be willing to consult with you about your particular situation, and he or she should express an interest and curiosity regarding your affairs. If you meet with an attorney and find that he or she does not have these qualities or isn't sympathetic to your desires, find someone else. In making your selection, do not be terribly concerned about the attorney's fees. If the attorney you like charges a few hundred dollars more than the one who doesn't seem to have time for you, spending the extra money will be well worth the results you will receive. This is not a time to be penny wise and dollar foolish. At the same time, just because an attorney has an expensive office and charges exorbitant fees, this does not mean you will receive bet-

ter service. The best thing to rely on when making this choice is your own personal judgment and your instincts.

5) DO ask for your attorney's help in deciding on the right tools for your estate plan.

<u>One size does not fit all in the estate planning field</u>. While something is always better than doing nothing at all, there is a wide array of options, ranging from a simple letter to elaborate offshore tax planning. While we favor the revocable living trust for most people, there are always exceptions. Some estates may not require this kind of trust, and others should use the revocable living trust only as a starting point. Your estate planner has the professional knowledge to put you into the proper vehicle(s). If you have chosen your attorney wisely, you can rely on his or her judgment to prepare the proper documents.

6) DO choose your trustee or your personal representative carefully.

If you have a trust prepared, the person who will manage your estate after you die is called a trustee. If you have a will, it is a personal representative who oversees the distribution of your estate. In either case, that person will have a great influence on the quality of your last impression. Review the chapter on "Choosing Your Trustee." Using the criteria in that chapter, make the best choice you can. Explain to your heirs why you selected the trustee or personal representative you have.

7) DO leave clear, positive instructions about your last wishes.

Your trustee or your personal representative is your ambassador to your heirs. You will be on the other side and won't be able to deliver the message yourself. Your ambassador must know your mind and must be willing to faithfully carry out your instructions. Make sure your attitudes and your wishes are clear, concise, unmistakable, and as positive as possible so your communication comes across the way you would want. The last thing you would want is for your last communication to cause a family feud when you intended to send love, peace, and solace to your heirs.

8) DO make a full disclosure of your plans.
An open and honest discussion with your heirs regarding your distribution plans is often the best approach. Your heirs know you are going to die, but they may not know what that means in terms of their inheritance. Before moving to the issues of money and property, set the proper tone by expressing your desires for peace and harmony and your loving intentions toward each of them. Explain that you have thought about these matters and have definite goals in mind but that you need input from them, as your heirs, if you are going to achieve your goals. Be straightforward, not coy or evasive. Don't make your heirs guess your true intentions. Lay out your decisions and the reasons for those decisions. If you will plan a time and then actually sit down to do this, you may find this to be one of the most richly rewarding times you have ever spent with your children or your other heirs.

9) DO place all your assets in the trust.
Always include all assets in your trust, unless your attorney instructs you otherwise (and, if that happens, you will want to fully understand why you are being told to keep an asset separate). The reason for including all assets is simple: If everything is in one place, there will be no unintended surprises or lopsided

distributions. The trustee is responsible for marshaling all the assets of your estate, including any that were unintentionally left out of your trust. Putting all of your assets in the trust and maintaining them that way, as well as titling new assets to the trust, makes your trustee's job much easier.

10) DO instruct your attorney to use loving language.
We have given a few examples in this book of the kind of loving language that can make a big difference in the way your last communication is received. You can apply these examples to your particular situation, adding your own excellent ideas and your own personal wording. The results will be much more satisfying than if you simply focus on the legal aspects of your transfer. Economically, the results of the two approaches may be entirely the same. However, we are human beings with feelings, emotions, heritages, and legacies to be considered. <u>Heirs are so much poorer, whatever the size of the estate, if all they receive are the material goods of their forebears.</u>

11) DO leave love letters.
Your loved ones will naturally grieve, but they needn't be left with an open emotional sore that never seems to heal. Do not let your spouse, your children, or any other loved ones wonder how you felt about them. Take the time to put your thoughts in a letter, sending your heirs a message of love and comfort that will soften their loss at your death. Share with them your precious memories, your most intimate thoughts, and your happy memories of spending days in their presence.

There is probably not room in the distribution section of your will or trust to place all of this correspondence, so write these letters in addition to your loving distribution instructions. Don't file them in some drawer. Put the letters with your estate planning documents, give them to your attorney for delivery, or put them in your safe deposit box. Do whatever you can to make sure your heirs will receive your letters of love after you are gone.

12) DO consider a gift to your favorite charity.
We believe we each become who we are largely because of the gifts, wisdom, and support we receive from our fellow human beings. Many of the gifts we receive in our lifetimes come from people totally unrelated to us. We suggest you consider passing those gifts on. Show your heirs that you belong to and believe in the entire human family, not just a nuclear group. We are convinced that this demonstration from you will make your heirs better people as well.

The DON'T List

1) DON'T procrastinate.
Just like the funny motto says: "Eat dessert first; you never know!" Make your plan NOW. Don't wait until you are under a lot of stress, until you are terminally ill, or until a friend or close relative dies. At that point, you may not be thinking as clearly as you would have been at an earlier, less stressful time. Consider this book your wake-up call.

2) DON'T leave your plan up to the probate judge.
Probate is an aggravating, expensive, time-consuming, and completely unnecessary process. Probate will only happen to

your estate if you let it. You are now aware of the emotional and financial costs of probate to your heirs. You will actually be putting your heirs through a dreadful ordeal, for no reason, if you take no action to avoid having your estate go through probate. Not only is the probate process long and expensive, the resulting plan created by the state for your assets will rarely, if ever, be the one you would have chosen yourself. Don't throw your loved ones into this inheritance hell. Probate can be avoided simply and without a great deal of expense. All it takes is a little planning.

3) DON'T take advice on your plan from non-attorneys.
For estate planning, you need a professional attorney who devotes his or her entire practice, or a great portion of it, to this area of law. It is not recommended that you even rely on an attorney who predominately practices in some other area of law. Even more importantly, please remember that you are putting yourself and your heirs in the hands of a dangerous amateur if you use a so-called estate planner who is not an attorney at all. Your estate plan is a legal document, not an afterthought. It should never be just a quick way for a salesperson to make a living. An estate planning attorney has no axe to grind, is not trying to sell you something else, and is familiar with all legal aspects that may apply to you. Never take any action that has any bearing on what your heirs receive or how they receive it without checking it out completely with your estate planning attorney. Saving money in this area by using a non-attorney is probably the most expensive—and most lasting—mistake you could ever make.

4) DON'T leave assets out of your trust.

Unless it is a specific part of your plan and recommended by your estate planning attorney, don't leave assets outside of your trust. There are very few instances in which you would experience benefits in terms of the law or the tax consequences by leaving an asset out of your trust. On the contrary, unless your attorney gives you a sufficient legal reason for taking a different course, you should assume that everything you own should be included in your trust. Placing all of your assets in the trust keeps it simple; and <u>simple is better when it comes to estate planning.</u>

5) DON'T assume your heirs are okay with your plan.

Don't assume your heirs are okay with your plan, especially if you are planning an unequal distribution. Communicate with them and talk to them about how they really feel. Your heirs, especially if they are your children, may tell you what they think you want to hear. They may think they are being loyal to you, they may not want to appear greedy, or perhaps they haven't thought things through completely. When it comes to discussing these matters, fear can get in the way for many people. It is important that you get past that and past any other family secrets or hang-ups if you want to achieve the most satisfactory result. It is truly worth the effort to find out what any problems may be while you still have the opportunity to solve them.

6) DON'T be overly influenced by a child regarding the distribution of your estate.

The suggestion to avoid being influenced by a child regarding your estate may appear to be the opposite of the suggestion above, which advises discussing your planned distribution with your heirs. We really aren't presenting conflicting advice. What we are suggesting is that, unless you have an only child, you must be aware of ulterior motives each of your children may have in making their own case. This is especially true if the result of what one child wants would be unfair to another child or to other heirs you may have. We feel you should listen to your children and then examine your own desires, paying close attention to the gut feeling you may have about what you should do. Act from your heart with your best intentions and with the harmony of your family in mind. If one of your children appears to be sheltering you from the others in the guise of protecting you for one reason or another, be especially vigilant about the motives for this behavior.

7) DON'T use your distribution to punish or coerce your heirs. People sometimes use their estate plan to punish or manipulate their heirs. We do not feel this is appropriate under any circumstances, and it often creates resentment toward the giver. If you have such negative feelings about someone who is close enough to be an heir, it is much better to resolve those feelings through thoughtful communication and discourse during your lifetime. Your last act on this earth shouldn't be one that fosters or supports negative feelings of the past. Resolve disagreements, and then use your estate plan to leave only loving thoughts.

8) DON'T talk only to some beneficiaries but not to others. Communicate with all of your beneficiaries. Anyone who has a right to be one of your beneficiaries in the first place has the right to give you input about your plan. Some of the worst

results come from buying into the prejudices or secret agendas of one or two beneficiaries to the exclusion of others. If you cannot get honest and forthright input from each person in a family meeting, poll them separately. Do whatever is necessary to obtain the truth of the situation from each person's point of view.

9) DON'T be overly influenced by a child in selecting your trustee.

Just as it is important not to allow a child to influence your decisions about distribution, it is also important that you refrain from being unduly influenced by a child with respect to choosing your trustee. Talk to your estate planning attorney about the reasons for your selection. Discuss the benefits and the drawbacks of the person you would like to have to represent you. Explain to your attorney that you want your trustee to be the person who will create the most unity, peace and harmony—not necessarily the person with the best business sense. Ask the attorney to guide that person in the distribution if you feel that this guidance will be necessary or useful when the time comes.

10) DON'T choose a person who is too controlling or prejudiced as your trustee.

Even if a person has every other character trait you are looking for, if he or she is controlling or prejudiced, that can mean disastrous results in carrying out your plan. Select someone who displays more humility; shows more respect for the other beneficiaries and refrains from taking sides. You may even have to select a trustee outside the list of beneficiaries or outside the immediate family. However, you are far better off to have such a trustee than a family member who will create waves in the calmest seas.

11) DON'T be afraid.
Don't be afraid to take action. <u>These are your assets. You have worked hard for them, and you have the right to do with them as your heart dictates</u>. Carry forward with the most love and compassion you can muster. It is your plan. You have the final decision. Make the best choices you can, and let go of the results.

12) DON'T fail to leave a Perfect Last Impression.
When all is said and done, material things don't mean very much. In transferring your estate to your heirs, you are not simply passing on money and property. You are passing on yourself, the legacy you have created and the love you feel for those closest to you. With careful planning that comes from the most honest and loving intentions, you can create an estate plan that will communicate a legacy of love and will create the most perfect last impression.

Good luck and Godspeed. We know you can do it.

GLOSSARY OF TERMS

This glossary applies only to the subjects in this book, and therefore the definitions may not reflect definitions found in a standard dictionary. The authors have used their own definitions and those found in a Black's Law Dictionary, 8th edition. We hope that they will help you to better understand subjects treated in this book.

401K Plan—A type of qualified pension plan.

Administration of the Estate—The period between death and the distribution of the assets to the heirs, during which the assets are managed by the representative under the direction of the probate court.

Administration of the Trust: The management of a trust from its inception until final distribution under the direction of the trust's provisions.

Agent—One who acts on behalf of and with the authority of another.

Amend—To make a formal change to a trust.

Amendment—A formal change to the terms of an existing trust.

Appreciated Asset—An asset that has grown in value over its original cost basis; (example: Stock in ABC Corporation purchased 10 years ago for $10,000 is worth $100,000 on today's market; it has appreciated $90,000 in that period of time.)

Asset—Property owned that has monetary value.

Asset Protection—Legal methods used to protect a person's assets from creditors, unnecessary taxes and legal attack, such as lawsuits. The art of applying such methods.

Assignment—The transfer of rights and/or title to property

Bare Legal Title—Title to property without beneficial interest in it.

Barter—The trading of one kind of goods for another as distinct from trading for money.

Basis—Value of an asset computed by determining the amount paid for it, adding the cost of improvements and subtracting the tax write-offs taken to date.

Beneficiary—One who receives income or property from a trust either directly or indirectly.

Beneficiary Designation—Naming a beneficiary to receive automatic title to certain assets (bank accounts, life insurance proceeds, etc.) upon the death of the owner.

Blanket Assignment—Legal document that transfers title to all items in a designated category of assets without specifically identifying each separate asset.

Capital Gain—Increase in value over basis of a capital asset (such as stocks or real estate).

Capital Gains Tax—Tax assessed on a realized capital gain. "Realized" means that the asset has been transferred and the value received by the seller, who is then taxed.

Capital Improvements—Those improvements made that will permanently increase the value of the property. For example the addition of a room to a house would be a capital improvement, whereas carpets or drapes will wear out over a period of time and would not be considered a capital improvement.

Charitable Gift—A gift made to benefit a charitable organization.

Charitable Remainder Trust—An irrevocable trust giving lifetime benefits (income) to the grantor and naming a qualified charitable beneficiary to receive the estate at the death of the grantor.

Codicil—A formal change to the terms of an existing will.

Conservatee—One whom a probate court has determined to be incompetent to handle his/her own affairs.

Conservator—One appointed by the court to manage the assets of the estate and/or the person of the conservatee.

Conservator of the Estate—One appointed by the court to manage the assets of the estate and the monetary affairs of the conservatee.

Conservator of the Person—One appointed by the court to manage the health and the personal affairs of the conservatee.

Conservatorship—The period during which a person's affairs are handled by another person appointed by the court due to some disability.

Cost Basis—The amount that is originally paid for an asset, such as stock or real property, plus the amount of any capital improvements made to that asset during the period of ownership.

Constitutional Business Organization—Business entity based on the contention that United States taxes are illegal.

Constitutional Trust—A trust arrangement based on the contention that United States taxes are illegal.

Contesting a Will—The bringing of a legal action to object to the terms of a will.

Corporate Trustee—A corporation acting as a trustee.

Co-Trustees—More than one trustee appointed to serve at the same time.

Crummey Powers—A device used along with an irrevocable insurance trust to pay insurance premiums without having the insurance policy included in the estate. The name derives from a tax ruling issued to Mr. and Mrs. Crummey.

Decedent—A deceased person.

Declaration of Trust—A trust agreement or contract.

Dependent—One who depends on another for monetary support; used here in the context of a minor, an elderly parent, a ward or a conservatee.

Domestic Trust—Created within the jurisdiction and under the laws of the United States.

Donor: One who makes a gift.

Donee: The recipient of a gift.

Durable Power of Attorney—A legal document that confers certain rights on the agent to act on behalf of the principal in the event of the principal's incapacity during his/her lifetime; all powers of attorney expire on the death of the principal.

Durable Power of Attorney over Assets—A legal document appointing an agent to manage the assets of the principal in the event of the principal's incapacity.

Durable Power of Attorney over Health—A legal document appointing an agent to make health care decisions for the principal in the event of the principal's incapacity.

Equitable Rights—The rights to possession, use, control and enjoyment of property as opposed to legal title to the property.

Estate—The sum total of all assets and liabilities owned by a person.

Estate Plan—The use of legal documents and financial tools to maximize the benefits of and control the distribution of an estate.

Estate Planning Attorney—An attorney who specializes in the practice of estate planning.

Estate Tax—A tax paid by an estate before transfer to the heirs or beneficiaries.

Executor—A person who carries out the provisions of a will.

Executrix—A female executor.

Fair Market Value—The value of an asset, which would be paid by a willing buyer to a willing seller in an unprejudiced market.

Family Limited Partnership—A private limited partnership usually formed by family members for the purposes of minimizing inheritance tax and maximizing asset control and asset protection.

Fiduciary—One who acts on behalf of and in the best interests of a principal (for example a trustee); "fiduciary" comes from the Latin word "fides" meaning faith or trust; fiduciaries are held to very high standards when acting on behalf of their principal.

Funded—Holding tangible assets; a "funded" trust has had the title to assets transferred into it.

Funding a Trust—The act of transferring legal ownership of property to the trust.

Gift—The transfer of an asset from one party to another without payment of valuable consideration.

Gift Tax—A tax levied on the fair market value of a gift.

Gift Tax Exemption—An amount exempt from a gift tax.

Grantor—The creator of a trust; one who gifts assets to a trust.

Grant Deed—A legal document that passes title to real property and warrants that the grantor holds legal title to the property granted.

Heir—One who is entitled to inherit property.

Holographic Will—A will written entirely in the testator's own handwriting.

Incidence of Ownership—Rights of an owner to control or use property.

Individual Retirement Account (IRA)—A tax-deferred retirement account for an individual.

Inheritance—Property passed at the owner's death to those entitled to receive it.

Inheritance Tax—A tax levied on inherited property payable by the heir.

Institutional Trustee—A bank, trust company or other institution doing business as a trustee.

Insured—The person(s) whose life is the measurement for the pay out of insurance proceeds.

International Business Corporation (IBC)—A business corporation formed offshore.

Inter-Vivos Trust—A Latin phrase meaning "during lifetime"; therefore a lifetime trust.

Intestate—Not disposed of by a will; dying without leaving a will.

Irrevocable—A legal document whose terms cannot be changed or that cannot be dissolved except as provided for by the terms of the original trust agreement.

Irrevocable Life Insurance Trust (ILIT)—An irrevocable trust specifically designed to be funded with a life insurance policy (s); often used for wealth replacement.

Joint Tenancy (with rights of survivorship)—A form of real property ownership in which each owner has an undivided 100-percent ownership interest and the right of survivorship upon the death of the other joint tenant(s).

Joint Will—A single will entered into by a husband and wife.

Last-to-Die Policy—A life insurance policy that pays when the last insured dies.

Last Will and Testament—A legal document providing for the transfer of property to the designated heirs at the time of death; wills are subject to the approval of a probate court.

Life Insurance—A contract entered into between a person and an insurance company wherein for a certain amount of money paid during a person's lifetime, that person's estate will receive an agreed upon sum of money upon his/her death.

Lifetime Exemption—An amount exempt from federal estate tax; it may be used either during life or at the death of the person entitled to it.

Limited Liability Company (LLC)—A company that combines the asset protection benefits of a corporation with the financial benefits of a partnership.

Living Trust—A trust created during the lifetime of the trustor, as opposed to a testamentary trust; short-term for "revocable living trust."

Living Will (Physician's Directive)—A legal document that defines the principal's wishes with respect to extraordinary medical life support procedures.

Marshal Assets—Gather and account for the assets of a decedent's estate.

Mirror Will—Two separate wills entered into usually by husband and wife, which are identical in all terms and conditions.

Money—A common medium of exchange for goods or services.

Offshore Trust—A trust created outside the jurisdiction and laws of the United States.

Oral Will—A will expressed orally, typically from a deathbed.

Personal Representative—A person who is charged with carrying out the provisions of a will.

Physician's Directive—A legal document that defines the principal's wishes with respect to extraordinary medical life support procedures.

Pour Over Will—A will leaving assets to the trustee of the testator's trust.

Present Interest—An interest that a person has an immediate right to, as opposed to an interest in which the right to it does not vest until the happening of a certain event or circumstance.

Private Annuity—An annuity set up between family members or by a closely held company, as opposed to one offered by a licensed insurer.

Private Fiduciary—An individual (as opposed to a company), who acts professionally as a fiduciary.

Probate—A court procedure for transferring the property of a deceased person to his or her heirs.

Probate Court—A specific division of a state court having jurisdiction over matters affecting estates; among other functions these courts handle wills, trust disputes and estates of minors and incompetents and monitor the actions of guardians and conservators.

Probate Judge—The judge who presides over the matters before the probate court.

Probate Examiner—Licensed attorney who works in the probate court to research law, review cases under consideration and assist and advise the probate judges.

Pure Trust—A trust based on the contention that United States taxes are illegal.

Qualified Pension Plan-A preapproved IRS plan for the tax treatment of retirement benefits to employees.

Quitclaim Deed—A document that passes legal title to whatever interest the quitclaimer may own in a parcel of real property; for example if a quitclaimer only holds title to one-half of the property, that would be all that would be transferred to the new owner.

Remainderman—One who receives assets after specific distributions are made or after initial beneficiaries are no longer entitled to them.

Retirement Plans—An informal plan devised between a person and his/her financial advisor to determine how much money will be needed and available at retirement, or a formal IRS plan, approved by the government, most of which are tax deferred to assist people in accumulating wealth for their retirement years.

Revocable—A legal document that may be amended or dissolved.

Revocable Living Trust—A trust created during the lifetime of the trustor, which can be amended or dissolved.

Right of Survivorship—The persons on title who survive the decedent and automatically inherit his or her share of the property.

Simple Will—A legal document providing for the transfer of property to the designated heirs at the time of death, where everything is left outright to one beneficiary or one class of beneficiaries in equal shares; for example, "I leave all of my possessions to my wife, if she survives me; if not, to my children in equal shares."

Settlor—A person who creates a trust and places assets in it.

Special Needs Trust—A trust for the benefit of a person unable to provide or care for him/herself; prevents public benefits from being withdrawn.

Springing Power of Attorney—A power of attorney that does not become active until the happening of a certain event. For example the power of attorney is not valid until the principal is proven by two competent physicians to be unable to manage his own affairs.

Stepped-Up Basis—A change in basis to an increased value.

Successor Trustee—A trustee who replaces a previous trustee.

Tenants in Common—Joint ownership of property wherein each party owns a 100-percent undivided interest but may will their share to whomever they please upon death.

Testamentary Trust—A trust created upon death usually by provisions left in a will.

The Three-Year-Gift Rule—An IRS rule wherein gifts made within three years of the date of death may be included in the decedent's estate.

Transfer on Death (TOD) Agreement—An agreement wherein the asset is to be transferred upon the death of the principal to the designated heir.

True Durable Power of Attorney—A power of attorney that does not expire during the life of the principal as opposed to a power of attorney which has an expiration date.

Trust—An agreement, written or implied, wherein the trustee holds property for the benefit of himself/herself or another.

Trust Agreement—The legal document that spells out the terms and conditions under which the trust estate will be managed and distributed signed by the trustor and the trustee.

Trustee—The person who manages the assets of a trust and carries out the duties specified in the trust.

Trustor—The person who creates a trust and transfers assets to it.

Uniform Prudent Investor Act—Model legislation passed by the federal government requiring certain rules and guidelines be met by fiduciaries who handle investments for third parties; each state may adopt the act and operate under it as is or revise it to its own specifications so long as it meets the federal standards.

Unfunded—Containing no tangible assets; an "unfunded" trust does not contain tangible assets such as real estate, money or stocks but may contain intangible assets such as a life insurance policy.

Unlimited Marital Deduction—An IRS rule, wherein spouses may pass an unlimited amount of property to each other without a tax consequence.

Wealth Replacement—Insurance proceeds used to offset the loss to heirs when assets are gifted to charity.

Will—A plan for the distribution of assets to the heirs of the decedent; the plan must be approved by the probate court.

978-0-595-42542-6
0-595-42542-9

www.ingramcontent.com/pod-product-compliance
Lightning Source LLC
Chambersburg PA
CBHW030922180526
45163CB00002B/433